SCHOLAST

LITERACY SKI

CW00420166

Vocabulary
Year 5

TERMS AND CONDITIONS

IMPORTANT – PERMITTED USE AND WARNINGS – READ CAREFULLY BEFORE USING

Minimum system requirements:

- PC or Mac with CD-ROM drive (16x speed recommended) and 512MB RAM
- P4 or G4 processor
- Windows 2000/XP/Vista or Mac OSX 10.3 to 10.6

For all technical support queries, please phone Scholastic Customer Services on 0845 6039091.

Author
Sylvia Clements

Development editor
Rachel Mackinnon

Copy editor
Sarah Sodhi

Assistant editors
Alex Albrighton and Sarah Sodhi

**CD-ROM design and
development team**
Joy Monkhouse, Anna Oliwa,
Micky Pledge, Rebecca Male,
Allison Parry, James Courier,
Jim Peacock/Beehive Illustration

Series designers
Shelley Best and Anna Oliwa

Book layout
Quadrum Solutions Ltd

Illustrations
Woody Fox

Designed using Adobe Indesign
Published by Scholastic Ltd, Book End,
Range Road, Witney,
Oxfordshire OX29 0YD
www.scholastic.co.uk

Printed by Bell & Bain Ltd, Glasgow
Text © 2010 Sylvia Clements
© 2010 Scholastic Ltd
2 3 4 5 6 7 8 9   4 5 6 7 8 9

British Library Cataloguing-in-Publication Data
A catalogue record for this book is available from
the British Library.
ISBN 978-1407-10226-9

Mixed Sources
Product group from well-managed
forests and other controlled sources
www.fsc.org Cert no. TT-COC-002769
© 1996 Forest Stewardship Council
FSC

Acknowledgements

The publishers gratefully acknowledge permission to reproduce
the following copyright material:

David Higham Associates for the use of extracts from *The BFG*
by Roald Dahl © 1982, Roald Dahl (1982, Jonathan Cape).

Every effort has been made to trace copyright holders for the
works reproduced in this book, and the publishers apologise for
any inadvertent omissions.

Extracts from Primary National Strategy's Primary Framework for
Literacy (2006) http://nationalstrategies.standards.dcsf.gov.uk/
primary/primaryframework/ © Crown copyright. Reproduced under
the terms of the Click Use Licence.

Due to the nature of the web, we cannot guarantee the content or
links of any site mentioned. We strongly recommend that teachers
check websites before using them in the classroom.

Contents

Chapter 2
Word roots

Chapter 4
Cross-curricular vocabulary

Chapter 1
Synonyms and antonyms

Chapter 3
Grammar

Chapter 5
Fun with words

Introduction

Scholastic Literacy Skills: Vocabulary series

By the age of five most children have an active vocabulary of over 4000 words, according to David Crystal, a major contributor to our understanding of how language works. He suggests that children learn, on average, three or four new words a day, and that 'a child reading Roald Dahl stories at age nine is being exposed to over 10,000 different words' (How Language Works, 2005). It is obviously important that children continue to add to their personal lexicon in order to both understand and make themselves understood in many contexts. However, as Crystal also tells us, definitions for these new words are not learned straight away; children need time and opportunities for new words to be added to their vocabulary, which is where we, as teachers, have a vital role to play. The words and activities in this book have been specifically designed to support that role.

Teaching vocabulary

Year 5 children are beginning to use language to create specific effects in their writing and speaking and listening activities, such as creating atmosphere, persuasion, humour and characterisation. In order to achieve this it is essential that their vocabulary continues to grow – poor vocabulary will restrict the development of literacy skills. Year 5 children should have access to a wide range of quality fiction and non-fiction material as reading success will foster vocabulary growth. In turn, however, lack of vocabulary knowledge will inhibit reading comprehension, which will prevent access to advanced texts. Teaching vocabulary is key to the success of disadvantaged pupils, where parental practice has not facilitated a wide vocabulary. Year 5 children are gaining independent control of literacy and so it is essential that they are provided with the tools to progress this independence. By introducing and teaching pupils vocabulary, learning opportunities will be widened and academic failure can be avoided.

About the product

This book contains five chapters of activities for teaching vocabulary. Each chapter focuses on a different vocabulary area, and is organised into four sections with clear objectives, background information for the concepts taught, teaching ideas, and photocopiable pages for use in whole-class teaching, with groups or for independent work. Each chapter also has a poster, assessment, Word of the week section and Fun with words sections. The word bank at the end of the book provides banks of words to be used in games and other activities linked to this book.

Posters

Each chapter has one poster. These posters are related to the subject of the chapter and should be displayed and used for reference throughout the work on the chapter. The poster notes (on the chapter introduction page) offer suggestions for how they could be used. There are black and white versions in the book and full-colour versions on the CD-ROM for you to print out or display on your whiteboard.

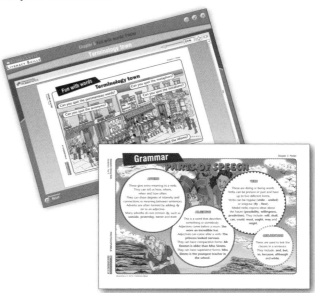

Assessment

Each chapter has an assessment section. It summarises the objectives and activities in the section, provides pointers on observation and record keeping and includes one assessment photocopiable page (which is also printable from the CD-ROM with answers, where appropriate).

Word of the week and Fun with words

For each chapter there are notes on Word of the week and Fun with words. Word of the week provides one word you might like to focus on related to each section. Fun with words provides general activities to use with your class throughout work on the chapter.

Word bank

The word bank at the end of each book provides a list of words you might like to use in games or other activities.

Activities

Each section contains three activities. These activities all take the form of a photocopiable page which is in the book.

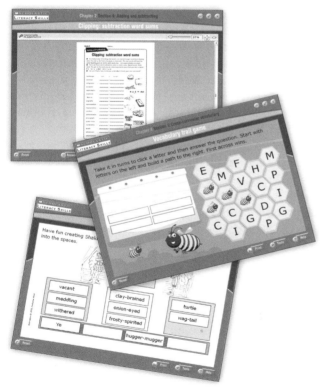

Each photocopiable page is also included on the CD-ROM for you to display or print out (these pages are also provided with answers where appropriate). Many of the photocopiable pages have linked interactive activities on the CD-ROM. These interactive activities are designed to act as starter activities to the lesson, giving whole-class support on the information being taught. However, they can work equally well as plenary activities, reviewing the work the children have just completed.

Differentiation

Activities in this book are not differentiated explicitly, although teacher notes may make suggestions for support or extension. Many of the activities can be used with the whole class with extra support provided through differentiated and open-ended questions, use of additional adults, mixed-ability paired or group work or additional input and consolidation before and/or after lessons. Some children may need support with the reading aspects of tasks in order to participate in the vocabulary objectives.

Using the CD-ROM

Below are brief guidance notes for using the CD-ROM. For more detailed information, see **How to use** on the start-up screen, or **Help** on the relevant screen for information about that page.

The CD-ROM follows the structure of the book and contains:

- All of the photocopiable pages.
- All of the poster pages in full colour.
- Photocopiable pages (with answers where appropriate).
- Thirty interactive on-screen activities linked to the photocopiable pages.

Getting started

To begin using the CD-ROM, simply place it in your CD- or DVD-ROM drive. Although the CD-ROM should auto-run, if it fails to do so, navigate to the drive and double-click on the red **Start** icon.

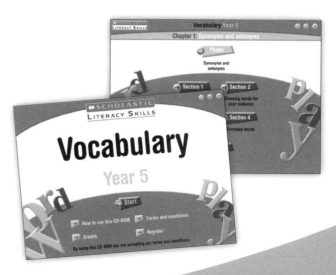

Start-up screen

The start-up screen is the first screen that appears. Here you can access: terms and conditions, registration links, how to use the CD-ROM and credits. If you agree to the terms and conditions, click **Start** to continue.

Main menu

The main menu provides links to all of the chapters or all of the resources. Clicking on the relevant **Chapter** icon will take you to the chapter screen where you can access the posters and the chapter's sections. Clicking on **All resources** will take you to a list of all the resources, where you can search by key word or chapter for a specific resource.

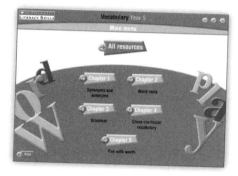

Section screen

Upon choosing a section from the chapter screen, you are taken to a list of resources for that section. Here you can access all of the photocopiable pages related to that section as well as the linked interactive activities.

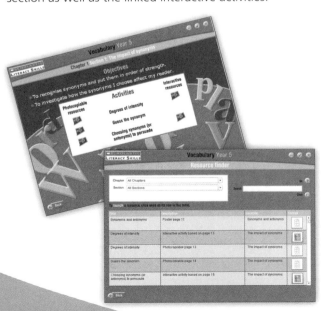

Resource finder

The **Resource finder** lists all of the resources on the CD-ROM. You can:
- Select a chapter and/or section by selecting the appropriate title from the drop-down menus.
- Search for key words by typing them into the search box.
- Scroll up or down the list of resources to locate the required resource.
- To launch a resource, simply click once on its row on the screen.

Navigation

The resources (poster pages, photocopiable pages and interactive activities) all open in separate windows on top of the menu screen. This means that you can have more than one resource open at the same time. To close a resource, click on the **x** in the top right-hand corner of the screen. To return to the menu screen you can either close or minimise a resource.

Closing a resource will not close the program. However, if you are in a menu screen, then clicking on the **x** will close the program. To return to a previous menu screen, you need to click on the **Back** button.

Whiteboard tools

The CD-ROM comes with its own set of whiteboard tools for use on any whiteboard. These include:
- Pen tool
- Highlighter tool
- Eraser
- Sticky note

Click on the **Tools** button at the foot of the screen to access these tools.

Printing

Print the resources by clicking on the Print button. The photocopiable pages print as full A4 portrait pages, but please note if you have a landscape photocopiable page or poster you need to set the orientation to landscape in your print preferences. The interactive activities will print what is on the screen. For a full A4 printout you need to set the orientation to landscape in your print preferences.

Framework objectives

Chapter	Page	Section	Literacy skills objectives	Strand 1: Use and explore different question types and different ways words are used, including in formal and informal contexts.	Strand 4: Use and recognise the impact of theatrical effects in drama.	Strand 6: Know and use less common prefixes and suffixes such as im-, ir-, -cian.	Strand 6: Group and classify words according to their spelling patterns and their meanings.	Strand 7: Distinguish between everyday use of words and their subject-specific use.	Strand 9: Experiment with different narrative form and styles to write their own stories.	Strand 9: Vary the pace and develop the viewpoint through the use of direct and reported speech, portrayal of action and selection of detail.
Chapter 1	12	The impact of synonyms	To recognise and order synonyms that have different degrees of intensity.			✓	✓		✓	✓
Chapter 1	16	Choosing words for your audience	To adapt vocabulary to meet the needs of a specific audience.	✓		✓	✓		✓	✓
Chapter 1	20	Alternatives for overused words	To select appropriate alternatives for *said* and *nice*, that give the audience more accurate information about intended meaning.			✓	✓		✓	✓
Chapter 1	24	Everyday words	To create synonym and antonym word banks to use in everyday writing. To improve the range of vocabulary used in everyday writing.	✓		✓	✓		✓	✓
Chapter 2	35	Investigating interesting and unusual affixes	To investigate the use and origins of unusual and interesting prefixes and suffixes. To use knowledge of suffix meanings to work out the definition of unfamiliar vocabulary.			✓	✓			
Chapter 2	39	Dig back to the roots	To learn to build words from known prefixes, roots and suffixes. To learn how to identify roots within words.			✓	✓			
Chapter 2	43	Will's words	To investigate words and phrases that William Shakespeare introduced into the English language.		✓	✓	✓			
Chapter 2	47	Adding and subtracting	To understand the origin of words that have been created by blending two words. To learn how words have been formed by back-formation or by shortening existing words.			✓	✓			
Chapter 3	58	Actively adding adverbs	To recognise and experiment with the positioning of adverbs in different locations in a sentence. To use adverbs to qualify verbs in writing dialogue.			✓	✓		✓	✓
Chapter 3	62	Amazing adjectives	To identify adjectives and understand the reason for their choice. To investigate and collect a wide range of ambitious adjectives to enhance creativity in writing.	✓		✓	✓		✓	✓
Chapter 3	66	Cooking up some verbs!	To understand the importance of verb choice when using the imperative. To investigate and use powerful verbs to create descriptions.	✓		✓	✓		✓	✓
Chapter 3	70	Complex connectives	To identify connectives and use more complex connectives in writing.	✓		✓	✓		✓	✓

Framework objectives

Page	Section	Literacy skills objectives	Strand 1: Use and explore different question types and different ways words are used, including in formal and informal contexts.	Strand 4: Use and recognise the impact of theatrical effects in drama.	Strand 6: Know and use less common prefixes and suffixes such as im-, ir-, -cian.	Strand 6: Group and classify words according to their spelling patterns and their meanings.	Strand 7: Distinguish between everyday use of words and their subject-specific use.	Strand 9: Experiment with different narrative form and styles to write their own stories.	Strand 9: Vary the pace and develop the viewpoint through the use of direct and reported speech, portrayal of action and selection of detail.
81	Making sense of science	To consolidate understanding of a range of scientific vocabulary. To consolidate specific science vocabulary.			✓	✓	✓	✓	✓
85	A world of words	To consolidate a range of geographical vocabulary. To use geographical vocabulary in group discussions.	✓		✓	✓	✓	✓	✓
89	Mastering maths talk	To consolidate and use mathematical vocabulary.			✓	✓	✓	✓	✓
93	Defining the past	To stimulate discussion and encourage the use of vocabulary associated with developing chronological awareness. To consolidate and use a range of historical vocabulary.	✓		✓	✓	✓	✓	✓
104	It's delumptious!	To deduce the meaning of made-up words and establish the word class. To use created words in narrative.		✓	✓	✓	✓		
108	Cut it short	To understand the terms *acronym* and *initialism*. To learn the origin and meaning of words that have been shortened or clipped. To experiment with more complex compound words.			✓	✓	✓		
112	Metaphorically speaking....	To consider the meanings of metaphorical expressions and idioms. To have fun explaining and illustrating oxymora.			✓	✓	✓		
116	Splish, splash, whoosh, whizz!	To experiment with onomatopoeia. To expand vocabulary relating to colour words and adjectives.			✓	✓	✓		

Chapter 4 (pages 81, 85, 89, 93)
Chapter 5 (pages 104, 108, 112, 116)

Using vocabulary

Using and developing children's vocabulary
Use these notes to support the teaching of vocabulary in this book.

EAL
It is important to remember that children learning EAL will vary in their understandings of the processes of additional language acquisition. In order to support children learning EAL you can sit them near the front, sit them with peers who speak the same first language but are more proficient in English, provide visual support in terms of pictures, drawings, photographs, videos and key words in print as well as utilising bilingual speakers and involving parents where possible.

Specific words
When tackling ambitious texts, in any curriculum area, it is advantageous to introduce specific new vocabulary before reading the text. This will facilitate improved comprehension and increase confidence and interest. Where the words are subject-specific, display them on walls or on word cards and revisit them in different contexts.

Word learning strategies
Children should be actively encouraged to use a dictionary or thesaurus on a daily basis. Ensure that dictionaries are accessible without requiring visits to bookshelves. Teach children to use the research facilities available as part of word processing packages. Provide a range of other dictionaries, such as etymological and rhyming dictionaries. When introducing specific vocabulary make reference to the various parts of the word, drawing attention to the root word and any prefixes and suffixes.

Concentrate on teaching three types of words
Important words: Teach the words that are essential for comprehension first. It is vital to prepare a text before a lesson, presenting important words on the board and briefly explaining them. In this way the lesson becomes more accessible to all children and will avoid the sense of failure children will feel if their lack of vocabulary prevents access to more advanced texts. Draw on the class's knowledge to help identify those children with a wider vocabulary. This will help with differentiating texts.

Useful words: Providing children with a bank of useful words before attempting independent writing tasks is a valuable support tool for all children. Before independent writing, discuss the types of words that the children may need for the task set. When sharing work during a plenary and when marking written work, give praise where children have adopted the newly introduced words.

Difficult words: Idiomatic and metaphorical expressions can present difficulties especially for children learning EAL. Take time to teach the implicit meanings and avoid using such phrases unless you back up their use with an explanation.

Word consciousness
A child's vocabulary is the set of words they use when communicating either orally or in writing. In order to incorporate new words they may need to enlist a series of techniques until the words are engrained, such as:
- using mind maps to draw relationships between different words
- using peer talk groups to discuss and use words in games
- using class dictionaries or word books to record and store vocabulary
- using mnemonics
- putting key words into stories
- using different colours to write key words.

Chapter 1

Synonyms and antonyms

Introduction

The aim of this chapter is to draw attention to the differences between synonyms, for example *angry*, *irritated*, *frustrated* and *upset*, and illustrate what impact the choice of word may have on the audience. The chapter addresses how synonyms can be used to replace overused words, such as *nice*, *said* and *good*, and draws attention to how careful word choice can make your meaning clearer. It also shows how the choice of synonym is important when adapting vocabulary for different purposes, for example, using more ambitious vocabulary when telling a traditional story to an older audience.

Poster notes

Synonyms and antonyms (page 11)
The poster provides definitions and examples of synonyms as well as tips and advice for checking whether synonym choice is accurate and appropriate. It provides an example of the possible implications that synonym choice may have. The poster can be used as a teaching tool while introducing the different activities or be produced as a large copy for display.

In this chapter

The impact of synonyms page 12	To recognise and order synonyms that have different degrees of intensity.
Choosing words for your audience page 16	To adapt vocabulary to meet the needs of a specific audience.
Alternatives for overused words page 20	To select appropriate alternatives for *said* and *nice*, that give the audience more accurate information about intended meaning.
Everyday words page 24	To create synonym and antonym word banks to use in everyday writing. To improve the range of vocabulary used in everyday writing.
Assessment page 28	Activities and ideas to assess the ability to use a thesaurus effectively to select appropriate alternative word choices.

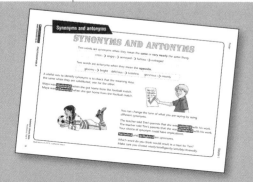

SYNONYMS AND ANTONYMS

Synonyms and antonyms

Two words are synonyms when they mean the **same** or **very nearly** the same thing.

cross ⬌ angry   annoyed ⬌ furious   furious ⬌ outraged

Two words are antonyms when they mean the **opposite**.

gloomy ⬌ bright   delicious ⬌ tasteless   generous ⬌ miserly

A useful way to identify synonyms is to check that the meaning stays the same when they are substituted, one for the other.

Maya was **shattered** when she got home from the football match.
Maya was **exhausted** when she got home from the football match.

You can change the tone of what you are saying by using different synonyms.

The teacher told Tim's parents that she was **satisfied** with his work.
The teacher told Tim's parents that she was **delighted** with his work.
Your choice of synonym could have implications.

Satisfied and **delighted** are synonyms.

Which word do you think would result in a treat for Tim?
Make sure you choose wisely/intelligently/sensibly/shrewdly.

The impact of synonyms

Objective

To recognise and order synonyms that have different degrees of intensity.

Background knowledge

We often understate and overstate situations through our choice of vocabulary. Sometimes our choice of adjective does not give a true picture of a situation: *This book was really good!* The word 'good' tells us little about the book. Was it an exciting thriller, or a heart-warming romance? Often we over-exaggerate a situation: *Corrrr, the sea is freezing!* Obviously it is not literally freezing. Perhaps 'really chilly' would be more precise.

Activities

This section uses drama and written work to explore the degrees of intensity of synonyms of commonly used words. Children will explore how the choice of synonym can have an impact on their audience.

● **Photocopiable page 13 'Degrees of intensity'**
The children will need a dictionary and a thesaurus. With a talking partner, ask the children to discuss the groups of synonyms and order them in degrees of intensity. Encourage the children to look up unfamiliar words and discuss situations where each word may be most appropriate. As a class, collect ideas for sentences incorporating the different words.

● **Photocopiable page 14 'Guess the synonym'**
Organise the children into groups of four or five and provide one set of action cards and two sets of synonym cards to each group. Let the children take it in turns to be the actor. The group should select an action and let the actor choose a synonym, highlighting it without the audience seeing. The actor should then perform the action in the manner of their highlighted synonym. The audience should decide which synonym has been used. The activity will focus attention on degrees of intensity.

● **Photocopiable page 15 'Choosing synonyms (or antonyms) to persuade'**
Carefully chosen synonyms can have an impact when writing to persuade an audience. The children need to carefully construct a letter requesting a resident to keep the Youth Club running. Highlight the need to be firm but polite. More confident learners can add further information to persuade the recipient, choosing their words carefully. Select some children to read their letters aloud and select another child to objectively select the most persuasive letter. Invite the children who added information to explain how they chose their words and which synonyms they selected.

Further ideas

● **Notices:** Ask the children to write notices and memos, selecting appropriate synonyms to create the intended impact. For example, a police notice warning people about an escaped prisoner or a headteacher's warning about playtime behaviour.

● **Thermometers:** Create synonym thermometers to display around the room with the most intense synonyms at the top, decreasing in intensity lower down the thermometer scale.

 What's on the CD-ROM

On the CD-ROM you will find:
● Printable versions of all three photocopiable pages.
● Interactive versions of 'Degrees of intensity' and 'Choosing synonyms (or antonyms) to persuade'.

The impact of synonyms

Degrees of intensity

■ Read the groups of synonyms in each box and look up any new words.

■ Decide which word has the strongest meaning and then sort the words in order, starting with the strongest at number one.

■ There is no exact right or wrong answer – it is open to debate.

Happy words		Cold words	
pleased	1 _____	chilly	1 _____
satisfied	2 _____	freezing	2 _____
delighted	3 _____	bitter	3 _____
thrilled	4 _____	Arctic	4 _____
ecstatic	5 _____	nippy	5 _____
overjoyed	6 _____	cool	6 _____
contented	7 _____	raw	7 _____
happy	8 _____	frosty	8 _____
Big words		**Tired words**	
huge	1 _____	sleepy	1 _____
large	2 _____	drowsy	2 _____
immense	3 _____	exhausted	3 _____
immeasurable	4 _____	weary	4 _____
vast	5 _____	shattered	5 _____
colossal	6 _____	fatigued	6 _____
infinite	7 _____	lethargic	7 _____
big	8 _____	somnolent	8 _____

Name:

The impact of synonyms

Guess the synonym

Action cards

■ Cut out the action cards below.

Show your reaction as you open the best ever birthday present.	Show your reaction as you go into the sea for a swim.	Show your reaction as you open a letter and receive bad news.	Show your reaction as you walk down a dark alleyway.
Show your reaction as you finish your PE lesson.	Show your reaction while you are waiting for your friend to arrive to go on a special day out.	You are a show-off. Show your reaction as you and your pet are presented with a trophy for Best Pet in Show.	You have missed the bus and have an exam. Show your reaction when your friend's mum offers you a lift.

Synonym cards

■ If you are the actor, highlight the word you are going to perform the action in the manner of. Remember not to let the audience see.

■ If you are the audience, watch the actor and choose the word you think they are acting out.

Set 1	pleased	contented	thrilled	ecstatic
Set 2	cool	nippy	bitter	raw
Set 3	disappointed	upset	distressed	distraught
Set 4	apprehensive	scared	terrified	petrified
Set 5	weary	fatigued	exhausted	shattered
Set 6	impatient	eager	fervent	enthusiastic
Set 7	proud	conceited	arrogant	haughty
Set 8	grateful	appreciative	indebted	obliged

The impact of synonyms

Choosing synonyms (or antonyms) to persuade

■ Rewrite this letter in your best handwriting, selecting the most appropriate synonyms from the ones in brackets.

■ When choosing, consider which synonym will be the most persuasive. If your synonyms are too extreme you will risk upsetting the recipient, if you are too reasonable you will risk having no impact at all.

63 Conifer Lane
Lower Hillside
Shottesford
CV43 3GY

28th February 2010

Dear Mr Bruce

I am writing on behalf of myself and the other children in the village of Lower Hillside to (**politely/respectfully/angrily/furiously**) (**request/demand/insist/beg**) that you do not close down our Youth Club.

Closure of the Youth Club would be most (**distressing/disappointing/upsetting**) for the children as it gives them somewhere warm and safe to play and meet up. We (**understand/appreciate/recognise/comprehend**) that running the Youth Club involves time and effort and some cost but we are prepared to contribute each week and will (**willingly/gladly/eagerly**) volunteer to help with the smooth running of the club by clearing away and washing up – we could organise a rota.

Surely you must (**appreciate/comprehend/grasp/recognise/understand**) the impact that taking away this activity would have on the children of the village?

We really must ask you to (**reflect on/consider/contemplate**) the effects of this action and find an alternative solution.

We (**look forward to/anticipate/expect**) your positive response to this polite request.

Yours (**beseechingly/imploringly/respectfully/demandingly**)

Charlie Forester

Illustrations © 2010, Catherine Ward.

Choosing words for your audience

Objective

To adapt vocabulary to meet the needs of a specific audience.

Background knowledge

Aesop's Fables are accredited to a storyteller who was purportedly a slave in Ancient Greece around the year 620 BC. The fables, which usually involve anthropomorphic animals, are widely used in teaching morals to children. By studying these stories, the children will become aware of the need to use different vocabulary for different audiences.

Activities

This section encourages the children to become aware of the need to vary their vocabulary choices to meet the needs of their audience.

● **Photocopiable page 17 'The Tortoise and the Hare'**

'The Tortoise and the Hare' is presented in very simple language. Ask the children to rewrite the story for an older audience, using more challenging vocabulary. The word bank provides synonyms for the verbs, adjectives, adverbs and nouns in the story. Discuss the meanings of the words in the word bank and ask the children to incorporate some of these words into their adaptation.

● **Photocopiable page 18 'The Lion and the Mouse'**

Aesop's Fables have been told for more than 2500 years. Show the children historical versions of the fables, such as Caxton's in 1484. Explain that as language changes over time, there is a need for new adaptations.

Ask them to rewrite a version of 'The Lion and the Mouse' for Key Stage 1 children. They should highlight any words that can be simplified and find alternative synonyms using a thesaurus or their own knowledge. Share the finished stories. Do they all convey the same meaning?

● **Photocopiable page 19 'Storytelling for different audiences'**

This can be carried out as either a written activity or a speaking and listening activity. For speaking and listening, enlarge, laminate and cut out individual synonym cards. Spread them face up in the centre of the circle of children. Invite the children to take turns to match pairs of synonyms. Tell the fable of 'The Fox and the Grapes' asking the children to think about which words on the cards they could use to retell the tale. Let the children take turns to tell the tale, turning over the cards as they are used. Then retell the tale for an older audience, using the more advanced vocabulary choices.

Further ideas

● **Paintings:** Ask the children to write a description of a famous painting for a young person and then use a thesaurus to source more adventurous vocabulary for an older person.

● **Museum labels:** Using your current history topic, let the children create museum labels of artefacts for child visitors and for adult visitors.

 **What's on the CD-ROM**

On the CD-ROM you will find:
● Printable versions of all three photocopiable pages.
● Answers to 'Storytelling for different audiences'.
● Interactive versions of 'The Lion and the Mouse' and 'Storytelling for different audiences'.

Choosing words for your audience

The Tortoise and the Hare

■ Rewrite this story in your own words for an older audience, choosing synonyms from the word bank below.

Once upon a time, there was a big-headed hare who boasted about how fast he could run. The tortoise, who was fed up of hearing the hare talk about how great he was, asked him to have a race.

"Even though you are so fast, I will beat you!" said the tortoise. The hare, thinking the tortoise was mad, agreed to the race.

All the animals from the forest came to the starting line to watch.

"Ready, steady, go!" The hare sprinted away from the start line and was off down the road, while the tortoise walked along slowly and steadily.

Turning to see the tortoise moving so slowly, so far behind him, the hare lay down by the side of the path and fell asleep, thinking to himself, "There's plenty of time for a rest."

Meanwhile, the tortoise carried on walking, slowly and steadily, never stopping until he reached the finish line. The animals cheered so loudly that the hare was woken from his sleep. He got up and began to sprint towards the finish but it was too late. The slow, steady tortoise had already won the race.

The moral of this story is, slow but steady wins the race.

Verbs	to ridicule, to be exasperated, to challenge, to affirm, to assent, to believe, to trudge, to continue, to persevere, to rouse
Adjectives	conceited, agile, incredible, swift, jubilant, raucous, victorious
Adverbs	resolutely, doggedly, comfortable, haughtily, relentlessly, promptly
Nouns	assertion, proposal, slumber, snooze, ovation, applause

Illustrations © 2010, Catherine Ward.

Name:

Choosing words for your audience

The Lion and the Mouse

■ Read this version of 'The Lion and the Mouse', written in 1884.

■ Underline words that you feel are too advanced for a Year 1 or 2 audience and record them in the box below.

■ Use a thesaurus to find simpler synonyms for these words and then rewrite the story for a younger audience.

A lion was awakened from sleep by a mouse running over his face. Rising up in anger, he caught him and was about to kill him, when the mouse piteously entreated, saying: "If you would only spare my life, I would be sure to repay your kindness." The lion laughed and let him go.

It happened shortly after this that the lion was caught by some hunters, who bound him by strong ropes to the ground. The mouse, recognising his roar, came up, gnawed the rope with his teeth and, setting him free, exclaimed: "You ridiculed the idea of my ever being able to help you, not expecting to receive from me any repayment of your favour; but now you know that it is possible for even a mouse to confer benefits on a lion."

The moral of this story is, no one is too weak to do good.

Words from the story	Alternative, simpler synonym
awakened	woke up

Choosing words for your audience

Storytelling for different audiences

■ Use the synonyms in the box to create one version of this fable for a younger audience and one version for an older audience.

■ When you have completed your stories, practise reading them with a partner. Listen to how word choice changes how the story reads.

The Fox and the Grapes

A **1** _____ fox **2** _____ a **3** _____ bunch of grapes

4 _____, **5** _____, on a grapevine. They were, however, so

high they were out of reach! He **6** _____ . He **7** _____.

He snapped. He reached as high as he could, **8** _____ with hunger as

he tried to **9** _____ them, but try as he might, he could not reach the

10 _____ prize.

   11 _____ by his failure to reach the grapes, he **12** _____,

with a shrug, to **13** _____ himself, "Oh, they were probably

sour anyway!"

   The moral of this story is, it is easy to **14** _____ what you can't have!

■ Which words are better for a younger audience?
■ Which words would be better for an older audience?

1	hungry	ravenous	8	dribbling	salivating
2	beheld	saw	9	snatch	seize
3	succulent	juicy	10	succulent	tasty
4	hanging	suspended	11	Upset	Thwarted
5	enticingly	temptingly	12	muttered	said
6	jumped	vaulted	13	comfort	console
7	bounded	leaped	14	hate	deride

Alternatives for overused words

To select appropriate alternatives for *said* and *nice*, that give the audience more accurate information about intended meaning.

The words *said* and *nice* are commonly overused words that are also rather imprecise. To communicate more effectively, help the children to find alternatives that are interesting and reflect what they really mean. Many children also choose weak verbs, such as *went*. With some careful thought, use of a thesaurus and by reinforcing how authors use words, the children will be able to use more powerful verbs to make their writing and speech more interesting.

These activities will encourage the children to think about using more interesting vocabulary in their writing. It will also help to increase their range of ambitious vocabulary.

● **Photocopiable page 21 'A superior word than said'**

Ask the children to read the dialogue and select an appropriate synonym for the verb *said*, crossing off each word as they use it. Draw attention to the fact that not all of the dialogue words come at the end of the speech. As a plenary, group the sentences according to the sentence structure. Discuss using *said* in conjunction with adverbs (such as *softly*, *quietly* and *angrily*) to more accurately express how dialogue is being conveyed.

● **Photocopiable page 22 'A niftier word than nice'**

Nice is a heavily overused and rather vague word. Encourage the children to consider alternative, more appropriate adjectives. After completing the cloze sentences, the children can write more sentences, using the word bank, to show that they have understood the difference an exciting choice of adjective can make.

● **Photocopiable page 23 'Punchy and powerful, not feeble and frail'**

Tell the children to read the whole sentence and then choose an alternative, more powerful verb from the word bank. Ask them to write out their revised sentences to give them a sense of ownership. Challenge the children who finish first to identify sentences in their reading books that could be improved by using a more powerful verb.

● **Avoid said:** Go to www.ngfl-cymru.org.uk and search for 'Don't use said' for a super slideshow presentation on avoiding using *said*.

● **Trees:** Display word trees around the class. When the children come across an unusual alternative for *nice*, *said* or *good* in their reading let them write it on a leaf and stick it on the appropriate tree.

● **Videos:** Film the children reading their sentences in the manners described on photocopiable page 21 'A superior word than said'. (Remember to get parents' or carers' permission before filming children.) Ask the children to guess which word describes how they are speaking.

On the CD-ROM you will find:
● Printable versions of all three photocopiable pages.
● Answers to all three photocopiable pages.
● Interactive versions of 'A superior word than said' and 'Punchy and powerful not feeble and frail'.

Alternatives for overused words

A superior word than said

■ You could use **said** in all these gaps, but that would be rather uninteresting. Liven up your dialogue with more ambitious word choices.

■ Choose words carefully to fill the gaps and maintain the meaning. Read all the sentences and the word bank before you begin to write. If you do not know a word – use a dictionary to look it up. You will not need all the words.

announced	bellowed	boasted	warned	declared
confessed	gasped	grumbled	sniffed	moaned	stammered
demanded	giggled	snorted	proclaimed	enquired

1. "I've got a terrible cold and I can't stop sneezing," _____ Ted, as he reached for yet another tissue.

2. "The mmmmonster – it's ccccoming to ggget usss!" _____ the gang as they turned and fled from the swamp.

3. The policeman shook his finger at the children, "Don't ever go near that railway embankment again," he _____.

4. "I've got so much homework," _____ Lisa, "I just won't have time to go to Jen's party."

5. The headteacher _____, "There will be a non-uniform day next Friday to raise money for charity."

6. "Get off my land!" _____ the farmer furiously.

7. "We're going to have another baby," _____ Dad, "and you're going to have a baby brother!"

8. "Our team is top of the league," Danny _____. "We're the best in the county!"

9. Pulling up her car alongside the village postman, the lost tourist _____, "Can you tell me the way to the Grand Hotel, please?"

Name:

Alternatives for overused words

A niftier word than nice

■ You could use **nice** in all the gaps, but that would be dull and unimaginative.

■ Choose words carefully to complete the gaps and maintain meaning. Read all the sentences and the word bank before you begin to write. You will not need all the words – use the remaining words to create your own sentences.

thoughtful   striking   unusual   appetising   pleasurable   considerate thrilling   relaxing   refreshing   charming   fascinating appropriate   breathtaking   magnificent   awesome

1. The nurse who cared for my grandmother was an extremely

   _____ person. She brought her cups of tea and

   took time to chat.

2. The journey along the coast in the convertible sports car was

   very _____.

3. After working out in the gym, Mandy liked a

   _____ dip in the spa.

4. The young man wore a very _____ suit for his

   interview – it was navy blue with a striped tie.

5. After the rugby match, the team were treated to an

   _____ snack of hotdogs with onion relish.

6. The young man showed that he was _____

   when he gave up his seat on the bus for the elderly lady.

7. There was a _____ view from the top of the Eiffel

   Tower.

8. The leaflet from the exhibition contained some

   _____ facts about all the exhibits.

Alternatives for overused words

Punchy and powerful, not feeble and frail

■ Verbs are the action words in sentences. Every true sentence has at least one.

■ Replace the verbs in bold in these sentences with more powerful examples from the word bank. Read each completed sentence to check for meaning.

materialised	skulked	sniggered	disembarked	scurried	selected
vanished	glimpsed	awarded	scrambled	flinched	administered
loitering	misappropriated	advised	accumulated	venture

1. The stunt rider **moved** away from the raging inferno that was once his motorbike.

2. The class **giggled** when Toby and Gemma were **picked** to be Romeo and Juliet.

3. The hamster **went** back into his nest when the cat **walked** past menacingly.

4. The little boy **backed away** when the nurse **gave him** his vaccination.

5. Henry sneakily **looked** over the teacher's shoulder to see what mark he had

   been **given**.

6. The tickets had been **stolen** and then sold to the unsuspecting public at a disproportionate price.

7. The obsessive collector had **built up** a collection of 6000 teapots of all shapes and sizes.

8. Peter loved playing on the edge of the forest but his grandfather **warned** him

   never to **go** out into the open meadow in case the wolf was **hanging** about.

Everyday words

To create synonym and antonym word banks to use in everyday writing. To improve the range of vocabulary used in everyday writing.

Background knowledge

It is easy to instil the habit of using dictionaries and thesauruses regularly, once children get used to the idea. This section focuses on making more ambitious vocabulary accessible to children, encouraging them to create their own desktop vocabulary mats to use during writing sessions.

Activities

These activities encourage the children to create banks of new adjectives and adverbs originating from known vocabulary, and demonstrate how to use these words. It would be useful to teach these before an extended narrative writing task.

● **Photocopiable page 25 'Adventurous adjectives'**
Encourage the children to complete the photocopiable sheet using thesauruses to identify useful, ambitious alternatives. They can do this individually, in pairs or as a group. When completed, laminate the photocopiable sheets to be used as desktop vocabulary mats.

● **Photocopiable page 26 'Astounding adverbs'**
Carry out this activity in the same way as photocopiable page 25 'Adventurous adjectives', collecting a wide range of synonyms and antonyms. Encourage the children to use some of the words they have found. While reading, if they find a sentence that they think

would be improved with one of their words, challenge them to write it out on the whiteboard and present it to the class. Reward children who actively seek to improve their vocabulary.

● **Photocopiable page 27 'Applying ambitious vocabulary'**
Model how to 'up level' a simple sentence. First, identify the different parts of speech in the sentence. Then decide where an adjective or adverb would improve the sentence. Discuss how to place the words in the sentence. Can the children replace the verb with a more powerful alternative? Challenge more confident learners to add a subordinate clause to change the sentence into a complex sentence. Invite the children to share their sentences. Can they alter the sentence using antonyms for the verbs, adjectives and adverbs?

Further ideas

● **Synonym sack:** Put objects with different textures in a sack. In a circle, ask the first child to take an object and choose an adjective to describe it: *This flower is delicate*. Invite the next child to suggest a synonym of the adjective, such as: *This flower is fragile*. Ask the next child to think of a new adjective and the following child to give it a synonym. If a child 'passes' they can either use the thesaurus or ask the rest of the class for an alternative to stay in the game.

● **Antonym sack:** Play a similar game with antonyms, where children give antonyms and say what the object is not. For example, *This flower is not robust*.

What's on the CD-ROM

On the CD-ROM you will find:
● Printable versions of all three photocopiable pages.

Name:

Everyday words

Adventurous adjectives

■ Write synonyms and antonyms for the words below.

Basic word	Super synonyms			Astonishing antonyms		
beautiful						
happy						
amazing						
angry						
marvellous						
horrible						
strange						
calm						
windy						
pleasant						
annoying						
great						
serious						
silly						
frightened						
loving						
excitable						
disappointed						

Name:

Everyday words

Astounding adverbs

■ Write synonyms and antonyms for the words below.

Basic word	Super synonyms			Astonishing antonyms		
sadly						
quietly						
strangely						
accidentally						
bravely						
quickly						
suddenly						
knowingly						
finally						
firstly						
crossly						
sincerely						
completely						
unfortunately						
excitedly						
carelessly						
apologetically						

Everyday words

Applying ambitious vocabulary

■ Use your vocabulary mats to add ambitious adjectives and astounding adverbs to these sentences. (Tip: try starting your sentence with an adverb.)

■ Replace the existing verb with a more powerful choice and improve the sentence. The first one has been done for you.

1. The dog ran across the road.

The excitable dog scampered

impulsively across the road

after the pretty, posh poodle.

2. The boy opened his present.

3. The man dropped his mug.

4. Alice looked at the monument.

5. Tom tore up his raffle ticket.

6. The weather was bad.

7. The troll shouted at the goats.

8. The pupil told his teacher he had not done his homework.

9. A bull appeared from behind the hedge.

10. The prince said that he would marry the princess.

Illustrations © 2010, Catherine Ward.

Assessment

Assessment grid

The following grid shows the main objectives and activities covered in this chapter. You can use the grid to locate activities that cover a particular focus that you are keen to monitor.

Objective	Page	Activity title
To recognise and order synonyms that have different degrees of intensity.	13 14 15	Degrees of intensity Guess the synonym Choosing synonyms (or antonyms) to persuade
To adapt vocabulary to meet the needs of a specific audience.	17 18 19	The Tortoise and the Hare The Lion and the Mouse Storytelling for different audiences
To select appropriate alternatives for *said* and *nice*, which give the audience more accurate information about intended meaning.	21 22 23	A superior word than said A niftier word than nice Punchy and powerful, not feeble and frail
To create synonym and antonym word banks to use in everyday writing.	25 26	Adventurous adjectives Astounding adverbs
To improve the range of vocabulary used in everyday writing.	27	Applying ambitious vocabulary

Observation and record keeping

Train children to read through their written work to identify words that could be replaced with more interesting or more powerful alternatives. Encourage them to put a neat line through words they are replacing and write the new word above. Explain that you want to see how they have thought about their choice of vocabulary. Record evidence of the children's use of synonyms and antonyms in their everyday writing against Writing Assessment Focus 7 (select ambitious and appropriate vocabulary).

Assessment activity

● **What you need**
Photocopiable page 29 'Wise word choices', writing materials, thesauruses.
● **What to do**
Ask the children to work individually to find three synonyms for the highlighted word, identifying which one is the most appropriate. This activity will assess how well children can use a thesaurus and select appropriate vocabulary. They will also realise that not all thesaurus entries can be used as straight replacements – there are shades of meanings that make vocabulary choice a precise art.

Differentiation

● Provide less confident children with thesauruses that are suited to their ability.

Further learning

● **Thesauruses:** Small notebooks can be made into thesauruses. Encourage the children to create an index at the front and head up each page with a number and keyword, such as *said*, *nice*, *good*, and so on. Hold short thesaurus sessions at the start of registration or the end of a day where children can record new words. Encourage them to record examples as they come across them in their reading.

Assessment

Wise word choices

■ Use your thesaurus to find three alternative words for those highlighted in the text. Circle the one you think is the most appropriate.

1. The doctor had been working through the entire night and was very **tired**.

_____   _____   _____

2. Duncan did not attend school on Friday as he was feeling **ill**.

_____   _____   _____

3. Sophie was very **happy** when her auntie came for a surprise visit.

_____   _____   _____

4. The bomb disposal expert stayed perfectly **calm** as he disarmed the explosive device.

_____   _____   _____

5. After she had finished her milk, the baby gurgled **happily**.

_____   _____   _____

6. "Leave my brother alone!" shouted Harry **angrily**. "Go and pick on someone your own size!"

_____   _____   _____

7. Half asleep, John **went** into the bathroom to wash his face and wake himself up.

_____   _____   _____

8. The circus acrobats put on an **amazing** performance, which made the crowd gasp in anticipation.

_____   _____   _____

9. The exchange family prepared a lovely tea to create a **welcoming** atmosphere for their foreign visitors.

_____   _____   _____

I can use a thesaurus to find synonyms.   ☐

I can choose words carefully to ensure meaning is preserved.   ☐

Word of the week

The Word of the week pages provide information on one word linked to each section in the chapter. Each word is described in some of the following categories: word definition, word origin, word family, alternative words, fascinating facts and activities. Not all categories are relevant to every word.

You can use the words as a focus to support your work on the different sections of the chapter. For example, you could create a display around it. The information is a starting point for a word focus. The words could form part of your classroom living word bank.

You could also use the word of the week as a springboard to inspire children to think about or research fascinating facts about words, find interesting quotations and to encourage them to use dictionaries and thesauruses.

Miniature

- **Word definition:** An adjective meaning being on a very small scale. A noun meaning an object reduced in size. A verb meaning on a smaller scale.
- **Word origin:** From the Latin *minium*, meaning red lead.
- **Alternative words:** Baby, diminutive, little, miniscule, minute, petite, small, teeny, tiny, wee.
- **Fascinating facts:** Ancient manuscripts were decorated with red lead: a type of chemical used as a colouring material. The Latin for red lead was *minium*. In the Middle Ages a verb was created to describe decorating a manuscript: *miniare*. From this evolved the Italian noun *miniature*, which referred to the paintings in old manuscripts. The English adopted this word to mean a small painting and soon it turned into a synonym for the adjective *small*.
- **Activities:** This is a useful synonym for small. Encourage children to replace *small* with *miniature* in their narrative.

> **Linked section:**
> The impact of synonyms, page 12

Colossal

- **Word definition:** An adjective meaning extraordinarily great in size, extent, or degree.
- **Word origin:** Relating to a colossus (noun), which comes from the Greek *kolossos*, meaning a sculpture that is considerably larger than life-size.
- **Word family:** Noun: *colossus*.
- **Alternative words:** Elephantine, enormous, gargantuan, giant, gigantic, great, huge, humongous, immense, vast, very large.
- **Fascinating facts:** The ancient Greeks made many *colossi* (plural). The statue of Helios in Rhodes (more than 30 meters high) was considered to be one of the Seven Wonders of the World. The Statue of Liberty in New York Harbour is a modern example of a colossus.
- **Activities:** It is a far superior word than *big* and can be used in narrative. What a super word to describe a giant in fantasy stories, for example.

> **Linked section:**
> Choosing words for your audience, page 16

Nice

- **Word definition:** Adjective meaning pleasing, agreeable, delightful.
- **Word origin:** From the Latin *nescius*, meaning ignorant.
- **Word family:** Noun: *nicety*.
- **Alternative words:** Admirable, amiable, attractive, charming, cordial, delightful, friendly, genial, good, helpful, kind, lovely, pleasant, polite.
- **Fascinating facts:** *Nice* originally meant stupid, but when the English adopted it in the 13th century the meaning slowly changed from ignorant, to shy, to refined and then to mean pleasant.
- **Activities:** This word is very overused – encourage the children to use thesauruses to find alternatives.

> **Linked section:**
> Alternatives for overused words, page 20

Grotesque

- **Word definition:** Adjective meaning odd or unnatural in shape, appearance or character; fantastically ugly or absurd; bizarre.
- **Word origin:** From the Italian *grottesco*, meaning crypt decoration.
- **Word family:** Adverb: *grotesquely*; noun: *grotesqueness*.
- **Alternative words:** Abnormal, absurd, bizarre, deformed, distorted, extreme, fantastic, freakish, gross, ludicrous, malformed, monstrous, odd, outlandish, perverted, ridiculous, strange, unnatural, weird.
- **Fascinating facts:** The English adopted the word *grotto* from the Italian, and it is closely related to *crypt*. A grotto was an underground room beneath a house or church, which featured bizarre paintings that combined human, animal and plant forms all interwoven. The Italians called these pictures *pittura grottesca* and it was not long before the English adopted the term *grotesque* to refer to anything that was distorted or exaggerated in an unpleasant way.
- **Activities:** Many fairy stories deal with ugly creatures who become beautiful in the end, for example 'The Frog Prince', 'Beauty and the Beast' and 'The Ugly Duckling'. The children could write similar stories that involve a grotesque creature who becomes beautiful or learn to like their looks.

> **Linked section:**
> Everyday words, page 24

Fun with words

. . . .

Use these activities to support the vocabulary work in this chapter. They could be used as starter or plenary activities.

Synonym/antonym bingo

● Write 20 or 30 words down one side of the whiteboard, such as *happy*, *sad*, *big*, *terrible*, and so on. Create a large, empty nine-square grid in the middle of the board. Ask each child to draw a nine-square grid on their personal whiteboard and fill each square with a different word from the list. When everyone is ready, the caller (you or a child) calls out a synonym for one of the words in the list, such as *gigantic*. If a child has the synonym for the word called they cross out their word. The caller records the word they called on the class whiteboard list for reference. The first to get a row or full house wins. Check the winner's choices against the class grid. Repeat the game using antonyms.

Synonym ABC

● In groups, give the children a starter word, such as *scared*. Challenge the children to find a synonym for this word, using every letter of the alphabet. For example: *afraid*, *bothered*, *concerned*, *disturbed*, and so on. Time the activity and stop the children after ten minutes, for example. The group with the most letters of the alphabet covered with acceptable synonyms is the winner.

Crazy crosswords

● Give groups of four children a large sheet of paper, felt-tipped pens and a thesaurus. Ask the first child to write a starter word in capital letters, such as *COMFORTABLE*. Taking turns around the group, let each child add a synonym using any of the letters contained in the starter word. So you could add the word *secure* using the last 'e' in *comfortable*, as the second letter in *secure*. Continue playing until no more words can be added. Encourage the children to use the thesaurus to help them.

Synonym hangman

● Let the children work in pairs. Ask the first player to select a word using the thesaurus and draw the correct number of dashes (one for each letter). Let them give the second player a synonym clue. For example, if their word is *dependable*, they may say one clue is *reliable*. Invite the second player to guess letters in turn. Correct guesses are inserted on the appropriate dash and incorrect guesses add another piece to the hanged man. The second player can ask for another synonym clue at any point but this adds one mark to the hanged man.

Chapter 2

Word roots

Introduction

The aim of this chapter is to identify word roots and their derivations to help the children extend their vocabulary. The study of the origin of words or parts of words and how they came to their current meaning and form is known as *etymology*. In broad terms, the English language was originally brought to Britain by the Angles, the Saxons and the Jutes, who crossed the North Sea from Germanic countries. The English language as we know it today has its roots in Latin, with Viking raids and settlements contributing many Norse words. Norman invasions also added French words to what was then called Middle English.

Poster notes

English language influences (page 34)
The poster provides a simplified synopsis of the history of the origins of some of the words in the English language that we use today. You can use it as a teaching tool to link with work in history or as a starting point for research into word origins from different periods or influences. You could allocate the children a time period to research and collect words that appeared in our language during this time.

In this chapter

Investigating interesting and unusual affixes page 35	To investigate the use and origins of unusual and interesting prefixes and suffixes. To use knowledge of suffix meanings to work out the definition of unfamiliar vocabulary.
Dig back to the roots page 39	To learn to build words from known prefixes, roots and suffixes. To learn how to identify roots within words.
Will's words page 43	To investigate words and phrases that William Shakespeare introduced into the English language.
Adding and subtracting page 47	To understand the origin of words that have been created by blending two words. To learn how words have been formed by back-formation or by shortening existing words.
Assessment page 51	Activities and ideas to assess the ability to identify words containing prefixes and suffixes and to build real words using root words and known prefixes and suffixes.

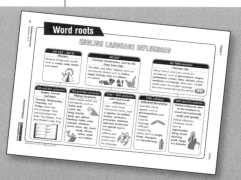

Word roots

ENGLISH LANGUAGE INFLUENCES

AD 122 – AD 41
Romans

Romans bring Latin words such as **camp, cook, kettle** and **street**.

AD 597
Christian missionaries, sent by the Pope from Italy

The Bible and other religious texts are introduced. Words such as **chalice, angel, bishop, font** and **album** are added.

AD 1066 onwards
Norman rule

Many French and Latin words are introduced, such as **government, mayor, parliament, crown, obey, dictate, chess, medicine** and **biscuit**. More than 10,000 words enter the English language from the French during this period.

5th and 6th centuries
Angles, Saxons and Jutes

Tuesday, Wednesday, Thursday and **Friday** come into the language. They commemorate the gods Tiw, Woden, Thor and Woden's wife, Frig.

7th and 8th centuries
Viking invasions

Some Norse words are introduced, such as **band, bull, crawl, die, drag, freckle, gasp, get, glitter, harbour, knife, raise, ransack, reindeer, scowl, sister, sky, stack, steak, thrust, want, weak** and **widow**.

15th – 18th centuries
Latin and Greek influences

Latin- and Greek-influenced words, such as **genius, incredible, lunatic, orchestra, prosecute, skeleton, spacious, testimony** and **gossip** appear. Prefixes, suffixes and compound words enter the language.

19th century
Industrial Revolution

Scientific words appear, such as **photosynthesis** and **cinema**. Colonial language infiltrates, introducing words such as **jungle, khaki, shampoo** and **boomerang**.

20th and 21st centuries
Global influences due to the freedom to travel internationally easily and quickly

Global influences introduce words such as **supermarket, bling, break dancing, punk, hippy** and **karaoke**.

Illustrations © 2010, Catherine Ward.

Investigating interesting and unusual affixes

Objectives

To investigate the use and origins of unusual and interesting prefixes and suffixes. To use knowledge of suffix meanings to work out the definition of unfamiliar vocabulary.

Background knowledge

Prefixes are added to the beginning of a base word to change its meaning. For example, adding 'anti-' (against) to the front of *septic* (to make rotten), creates *antiseptic* (counteracting sepsis by killing germs). Many prefixes originate from Latin and Greek. Suffixes are added to the end of a base word to slightly change its meaning. For example, they may change the tense of a verb (*play – played*), or the word class (*rely – reliable*). Suffixes often have implications for the spelling of the base word.

Activities

Understanding the meanings of a range of prefixes and suffixes is an excellent way to increase the range of known vocabulary. The activities are divided into Greek and Latin prefixes to help children understand the origin of words.

● **Photocopiable page 36 'Latin prefixes'**
As a class, discuss the meaning of the Latin prefixes. Create a spider diagram of words the children know containing each prefix to establish and consolidate the meaning of each. This will help children with a restricted vocabulary when they start the independent task. Let the children use dictionaries to match prefixes and base words to create complete words and definitions. Invite them to add another word containing the prefix and check their understanding of the word, ready to share in the plenary.

● **Photocopiable page 37 'Greek prefixes'**
As a class, study the Greek prefix table. Discuss any words the children are familiar with and record these on the board. Let the children use the prefix definitions to match the words to their definitions. They can check in a dictionary. Children should then find other words containing the prefixes and make definitions to test the class with during the plenary session.

● **Photocopiable page 38 'Suffix matching game'**
Cut out the word definition and vocabulary cards and place them face down on the table. Keep the suffix definition table for reference. Children work in pairs, taking turns to turn over and try to match the vocabulary and definition cards. Players keep matching pairs. The winner is the player with the most pairs.

Further ideas

● **Prefix word bank:** Give the children bright postcard-sized cards to create prefix word bank cards. Write the prefix in large letters on one side and add words on the back as they are discovered. Store them alphabetically.

● **Set in stone:** Make a display of a Roman amphitheatre or a Greek temple. Let the children decorate it with stones containing Latin or Greek derived words.

What's on the CD-ROM

On the CD-ROM you will find:
● Printable versions of all three photocopiable pages.
● Answers to all three photocopiable pages.
● Interactive versions of 'Latin prefixes' and 'Greek prefixes'.

Name:

Latin prefixes

■ Read the list of prefixes and their meanings. Now look at the base words and their meanings. Choose a prefix and match it to a base word. Write a definition for the word you have created (use a dictionary if you are unsure).

■ Can you add another word with the same prefix to your list?

Latin prefixes	Base words	New word	Definition	Extra word
aque- (water)	merge			
un- (not)	body			
trans- (across)	used			
dis- (apart)	script			
anti- (against)	duct			
post- (after or behind)	sonic			
sub- (under)	Atlantic			
super- (above)	sect			
bi- (two)	necessary			
circum- (around)	stance			

Greek prefixes

■ Read the list of Greek prefixes, their definitions and an example of a word containing each prefix. Use this information to match the words to the definitions in the table below.

■ Can you find another word containing each of the prefixes and write a sentence containing the word?

Greek root	Basic meaning	Example word
anthrop-	human	anthropology
chron-	time	chronicle
dem-	people	demography
dia-	through/across	diagonal
mono-	one/single/alone	monotone
morph-	form	morphology
-path-	feeling/suffering	sympathy
philo-/phil-	loving/having an attraction to	philharmonic
-phon-	sound	cacophony
para-	from/beside	parasite

1. The name for the study of human beings and their evolution:

_____

2. A sound that is continuous or repeated on one note: _____

3. A record of events in time order of happening: _____

4. A plant or animal feeding from or on another: _____

5. A harsh, clashing sound: _____

6. Devoted to music: _____

7. Feeling sorrow for another person's pain: _____

8. In biology, the study of the form of organisms: _____

9. A line that joins two opposite angles, running across or through

a shape: _____

10. The study of human populations: _____

Illustrations © 2010, Catherine Ward.

Name:

Investigating interesting and unusual affixes

Suffix matching game

■ Cut out the word definition and vocabulary cards and place them face down. In pairs, take it in turns to turn over one word card and one suffix card. If the cards match then you get to keep the pair. Use the suffix definition table to help you.

Suffix definition table

Suffix	Meaning
-ist	practising a particular skill or study
-gram	written or drawn
-graph	an instrument for writing, drawing or recording
-logue	speech
-oid	like/resembling and shape/form (forms adjectives and nouns)
-phile	one that loves or has a strong affinity for/loving
-arium	a place for

Word definitions

Like a human	A drawn record of heartbeats
3D object that is shaped like a ball	Someone who loves and collects books
A device for recording the size of an earthquake	An enclosed container for growing and displaying live animals or plants
A speech or play for one actor	A glass-sided tank where water animals are kept
A person who studies behaviour	A lover of France and all things French

Vocabulary cards

humanoid	psychologist
xenophobia	cardiogram
arachnophobia	bibliophile
spheroid	terrarium
seismograph	aquarium
monologue	Francophile

Dig back to the roots

Objectives

To learn to build words from known prefixes, roots and suffixes. To learn how to identify roots within words.

Background knowledge

A morpheme is the smallest linguistic unit that has meaning. For example, *unhelpful* consists of the morphemes *un-*, *help* and *-ful*. *Un* and *ful* are bound morphemes – they are not words in their own rights. However, *help* is a free morpheme as it is a word in its own right. Roots, such as *rupt* (meaning break) and *ignis* (meaning fire) are derivational but not actual words, however, they do still form word roots.

Activities

These activities encourage children to identify the word roots. It is not necessary to use the term *morphemes* with the children.

● **Photocopiable page 40 'Building from the roots'**
Explain that many words are made up of a root plus prefixes and suffixes. Invite the children to work with a talk partner and dictionary to collect words that contain the roots on the photocopiable sheet. Share the first example and discuss the words that are given. Can they disassemble the words and identify the prefixes and suffixes?

● **Photocopiable page 41 'Back to the roots'**
Display a set of words on the board, such as *signal*, *signature*, *design*, *insignia* and *significant*. Can the children identify the common root? (*Sign* or *signi*.) Discuss the meaning of each word, using an online dictionary on the whiteboard if necessary. Establish a

meaning for the root by deciding what each definition has in common. (Sign, mark or seal.) Explain that these roots are derivations and do not necessarily form words that will stand alone as words (unlike in the previous activity). Let the children work with a talk partner to carry out the same activity for the groups of words on the photocopiable sheet.

● **Photocopiable page 42 'Be afraid…be very afraid'**
The word *phobia* comes from the ancient Greek word *phobos*, meaning a great fear. Children may be familiar with terms such as *arachnophobia* (fear of spiders). By combining Latin or Greek roots with this root word, they can invent new words. This shows clearly how words from Greek and Latin origins are combined to create the words that we use today.

Further ideas

● **Game on:** Set up www.prefixsuffix.com as a favourite on the class computer. Direct children to the root search facility. Invite them to have a go at the site's vocabulary games.

● **Root race:** Put up a root word such as *colour* and challenge the children to come up with as many words as possible in pairs using the root, such as *discolouration*, *colourful*, *colouring*, *colourless* and *colourfully*. Share answers and praise new ambitious examples.

What's on the CD-ROM

On the CD-ROM you will find:
● Printable versions of all three photocopiable pages.
● Answers to 'Back to the roots' and 'Be afraid…be very afraid'.
● Interactive version of 'Building from the roots'.

Name:

Dig back to the roots

Building from the roots

■ Work with a partner to discuss and look up words that contain the following roots. The first one has been done for you.

1. sign (from the Latin **signum**, meaning 'a mark')

insignificant, significant, signature, signal, signify

2. act (from the Latin **acta**, meaning 'to act or perform')

3. audit (from the Latin **auditus**, meaning 'an act of hearing')

_____

4. tact (from the Latin **tactus**, meaning 'a sense of touch')

_____

5. photo (from the Greek **phos**, meaning 'light')

_____

6. auto (from the Greek **autos**, meaning 'self')

_____

7. potent (from the Latin **potent**, meaning 'powerful')

_____

8. press (from the Latin **pressare**, meaning 'to keep pressing')

_____

9. scribe (from the Latin **scriber**, meaning 'to write')

_____

10. comic (from the Greek **komos**, meaning 'having fun')

_____

■ Using the origin of the root and your knowledge of prefixes and suffixes, try to work out the meanings of the words you have found. It is like piecing together a jigsaw puzzle – once you have all the pieces you can see the whole picture.

■ Choose one new word and put it into a sentence to show its meaning.

_____

Dig back to the roots

Back to the roots

■ These roots come from Latin or Greek, but do not form real words that we would use on their own. Read each set of three words that all contain the same root and find a definition for each word. Work out what they have in common to discover the meaning of the root word.

■ Can you find one more word for each root you have investigated?

Word	Meaning	Root and its meaning
interrupt		
rupture		
corrupt		
ignite		
ignition		
igneous		
rejection		
dejected		
trajectory		
injunction		
conjunction		
juncture		
punctuation		
acupuncture		
puncture		

Name:

Dig back to the roots

Be afraid…be very afraid

■ The Greek word **phobos** means fear. In English we use the word **phobia** as a root word to mean a fear of something. It is used as a word in its own right.

■ We add on other root words that derive from Latin and Greek to create nouns that mean a fear or great dislike of something.

■ Read the Greek and Latin roots and their meanings. Use them to write a definition of the English word that has been created by joining the two root words. The first one has been done for you.

Root	Definition	Root	Definition
erythos	red (blushing)	graphe	writing
hippo	horse	ornithos	birds
myco	fungus	triskaideka	13
arachne	spiders	claustrum	enclosed space
pyr	fire	akros	that which is topmost
nycto	night/dark	hydro	water

1. Arachnophobia = *a fear of spiders*

2. Pyrophobia = _____

3. Claustrophobia = _____

4. Triskaidekaphobia = _____

5. Ornithophobia = _____

6. Erythrophobia = _____

7. Nyctophobia = _____

8. Hippophobia = _____

9. Mycophobia = _____

10. Graphophobia = _____

11. Acrophobia = _____

12. Hydrophobia = _____

Illustrations © 2010, Catherine Ward.

Will's words

Objective

To investigate words and phrases that William Shakespeare introduced into the English language.

Background knowledge

After the Normans conquered Britain in 1066, French and Latin were considered to be the languages of the educated person. English was considered a second-class language. However, English soon became the primary, respected language and was used in printed books. While the period of the late Tudors was a time of exploration, wars and colonisation that introduced many new words into English, people found that they simply did not have the vocabulary to describe and express their ideas. Shakespeare and other writers were responsible for introducing and recording many thousands of new words. The rules, grammar and spelling of English were not standardised formally until Shakespeare began writing his plays. Their popularity helped to standardise English into the form we know today.

Activities

Children are naturally inquisitive and will enjoy finding out what Shakespeare introduced and in doing so will expand their vocabulary further.

● **Photocopiable page 44 'Shakespearean words'**
Let the children use this wordsearch to find words introduced into English by Shakespeare. They should then sort the words into verbs and adjectives and check their definitions.

● **Photocopiable page 45 'Double, double toil and trouble'**
Copy the list of Shakespearean phrases, laminate and cut out. Make a large black paper cauldron to put the phrases in, explaining the origin of the quote from Macbeth. Ask a representative from each group to secretly pull a phrase from the cauldron, discuss its meaning with their group (clarify with an adult) and work out a short play or dialogue to present to the class, without using the words of the phrase. Invite the groups to research their phrases – the site www.phrases.org.uk is very useful. The groups should present their play for the audience to guess the expression. Challenge children to locate the expressions in the actual plays and then use the photocopiable sheet as a stimulus for writing short pieces of narrative incorporating the expression.

● **Photocopiable page 46 'To curse or not to curse'**
In Elizabethan times flowery, lavish insults were a sign of being articulate. Hand out the photocopiable sheet to groups and discuss the words in the four columns. Explain that the phrases they create will be formed from a pronoun, an adjective or two and finally a noun. Invite the children to incorporate their insults into Elizabethan-style mini-plays. Ensure they do not aim them at each other.

Further ideas

● **Shakespeare dictionary:** Create an online dictionary of Shakespeare's words that are still used today. Research where they appeared in his works and add this as an interesting page on the school website.

What's on the CD-ROM

On the CD-ROM you will find:
● Printable versions of all three photocopiable pages.
● Answers to 'Shakespearean words'.
● Interactive versions of 'Shakespearean words' and 'To curse or not to curse'.

Name:

Will's words

Shakespearean words

■ The word search below contains words that William Shakespeare introduced into the English language. They can all be found in his plays.

■ Find the words then sort them into verbs and adjectives. Use a dictionary to help you to find the meanings of new vocabulary. Write them on another sheet of paper. The first one has been done for you.

| dwindle | swagger | glow | tranquil | jaded | dishearten | mimic |
| majestic | laughable | barefaced | gnarled | frugal |

s	d	q	f	j	a	d	e	d	l	m	f
a	w	f	r	m	a	j	e	s	t	i	c
s	i	a	u	a	b	w	a	n	k	m	a
z	n	m	g	p	v	s	e	d	l	i	g
w	d	p	a	g	t	f	t	i	q	c	b
d	l	q	l	r	e	t	y	s	w	u	a
y	e	a	h	t	a	r	u	h	j	y	r
g	p	z	g	x	s	a	c	e	a	f	e
n	o	y	e	w	f	n	f	a	i	j	f
a	w	d	o	l	a	q	h	r	u	n	a
r	g	l	e	k	c	u	i	t	f	s	c
l	g	p	b	s	d	i	j	e	t	f	e
e	l	a	u	o	f	l	l	n	u	u	d
d	e	l	a	u	g	h	a	b	l	e	s

Verbs	Adjectives
dwindle: to decrease little by little to almost nothing.	

Will's words

Double, double toil and trouble

■ Read the summary of the origin of the expression, 'All that glisters is not gold' to find out how Shakespeare created this expression.

■ Can you describe a modern-day example of this expression?

All that glisters is not gold
(*The Merchant of Venice*)

Something flashy and showy may not necessarily be valuable.

Portia is a beautiful lady who is being pursued by many suitors, but she is not allowed to choose who she wishes to marry. Her late father stated in his will that she is to marry the man who correctly picks the casket that holds her picture.

There are three caskets: one casket is gold, another is silver, and the third is lead.

The Prince of Morocco is one suitor who tries to win Portia's hand, and he decides that because of her beauty, Portia could only have her portrait in a gold casket, and so he chooses that one. As he unlocks it, he is shocked to find a picture, not of Portia but of Death, with a message written in its hollow eye:

"All that glisters is not gold;
Often have you heard that told.
Many a man his life hath sold
But my outside to behold.
Gilded tombs do worms enfold."

The Prince quickly leaves Portia with a heavy heart.

■ Choose one of the expressions below and write a short paragraph to explain its meaning on another sheet of paper.

Shakespeare's expressions

Eaten out of house and home (*Henry IV Part II*)
A foregone conclusion (*Othello*)
As dead as a doornail (*King Henry VI*)
Love is blind (*The Merchant of Venice*)
More fool you (*The Taming of the Shrew*)
In stitches (*Twelfth Night*)
In a pickle (*The Tempest*)
At one fell swoop (*Macbeth*)
As good luck would have it (*The Merry Wives of Windsor*)
Green-eyed monster (*The Merchant of Venice* and *Othello*)

Illustrations © 2010, Catherine Ward.

Name:

Will's words

To curse or not to curse

■ Shakespeare used hundreds of insults formed from a variety of adjectives and nouns, many of which are no longer used today. Have fun experimenting with these Elizabethan terms, but only use them in the context of a play.

Thou art a boil, a plague sore, an embossed carbuncle in my corrupted blood. (*King Lear*)

■ Have a go at creating insults in the style of William Shakespeare.
■ Choose an Elizabethan pronoun from Box 1. Then choose an adjective from each of Boxes 2 and 3. Complete your insult with a noun from Box 4.

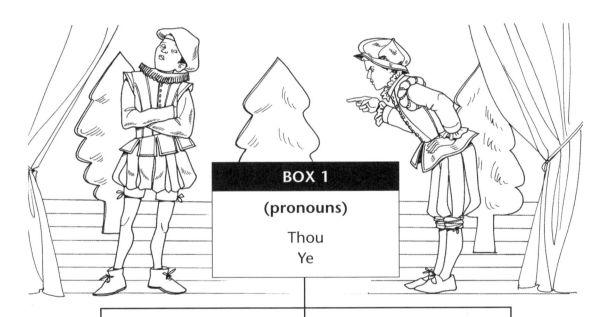

BOX 1

(pronouns)

Thou
Ye

BOX 2

(adjectives)

poisonous	waggish
rank	villainous
pribbling	jaded
yeasty	spongy
saucy	greasy
artless	dankish
vacant	withered
meddling	

BOX 3

(adjectives)

plume-plucked
knotty-pated
onion-eyed
rump-fed
white-livered
frosty-spirited
clay-brained

BOX 4

(nouns)

haggard flap-dragon
bog of guts measle
turtle
wag-tail
pantaloon barnacle
minnow addle-egg
clot pole hugger-mugger
hedge-pig boggler

My completed insult is: _____

Illustrations © 2010, Catherine Ward.

PHOTOCOPIABLE

■SCHOLASTIC
www.scholastic.co.uk

Adding and subtracting

Objectives

To understand the origin of words that have been created by blending two words. To learn how words have been formed by back-formation or by shortening existing words.

Background knowledge

A portmanteau is a travelling case made up of two halves, joined together by a hinge. It is also made of two words: the French *porter* (to carry) and *manteau* (a cloak). Portmanteau words are generally formed by joining the beginning of one word with the ending of a second, the two words having a common vowel. They were coined by Lewis Carroll in 1872. They are easily understood and an easy way of creating new words.

Another way to form new words from existing words is by back-formation – starting with a word that appears to have been formed with a suffix or prefix. For example, the noun *jelly* where the suffix 'y' is removed to form the new word *jell*, meaning to congeal or set.

Some words have their roots in the shortened form of existing ones. This is commonly achieved by removing either the first or last part of the word, or even both, as in *flu* (from *influenza*). This technique is called *clipping*. This differs from back-formation as the class of word generally stays the same.

Activities

These activities help children to appreciate the origin of a range of words that have been adapted or created through imaginative manipulation of the English language.

- **Photocopiable page 48 'Portmanteau: addition word sums'**
Explain the origin of portmanteau words. If the children know any, invite them to work out which two words they originate from. Collect a few examples before inviting the children to complete the sums on the photocopiable sheet. During the plenary, check the spellings of the words and discuss why the children think some of the words were created.
- **Photocopiable page 49 'Back-formation'**
Invite the children to create verbs from the list of nouns supplied to see how the words were invented. Can they then write sentences that demonstrate the meanings of the words?
- **Photocopiable page 50 'Clipping: subtraction word sums'**
Explain to the children that a common way of forming new words is to shorten longer words by removing either the end or the front of the word, or even both. Children should be familiar with most of the words, but may be unaware of the full-length version of the words.

Further ideas

- **Portmanteau challenge:** Set the challenge of finding 50 valid portmanteau words. Award a prize for the most imaginative list. Award an individual prize for any group that finds an example that no one else found. (This will prevent them simply copying from websites.)

What's on the CD-ROM

On the CD-ROM you will find:
- Printable versions of all three photocopiable pages.
- Answers to 'Portmanteau: addition word sums' and 'Clipping: subtraction word sums'.
- Interactive versions of 'Portmanteau: addition word sums' and 'Clipping: subtraction word sums'.

Name:

Portmanteau: addition word sums

In 1872, Lewis Carroll coined the term **portmanteau word**: two words that are joined using the start of one word and the end of another. The two words usually have a common vowel that is often shared. In 1843 the word **squirl** was invented by blending together the words **squiggle** and **whirl** (to describe a flourish in handwriting).

■ Try to work out these portmanteau words by blending together the two original words. Can you make up some of your own?

electronic + mail = _____

prim + sissy = _____

breakfast + lunch = _____

motor + hotel = _____

guess + estimate = _____

education + entertainment = _____

telephone + marathon = _____

parachute + trooper = _____

gigantic + enormous = _____

breath + analyser = _____

internal + communication = _____

outside + patient = _____

clap + crash = _____

fantastic + fabulous = _____

squirm + wiggle = _____

international + network = _____

blow + spurt = _____

bold + rash = _____

camera + recorder = _____

Adding and subtracting

Back-formation

■ James Murray was the editor of the Oxford English Dictionary in 1897. He coined the term **back-formation**, which means forming new words by removing suffixes or prefixes.

■ Choose ten of these nouns and use back-formation to create verbs from them.

■ Write the root verb for each new word and then write a sentence to demonstrate its use. The first one has been done for you.

Nouns			
babysitter	donation	injury	liaison
editor	escalator	kidnapper	orientation
diagnosis	gambler	shoplifter	surveillance

■ New verbs created by back-formation.

Verb	Sentence
To babysit	I had to babysit for my sister so she could go to the party.

Name:

Adding and subtracting

Clipping: subtraction word sums

■ A common way of forming new words is to shorten longer words by removing either the end or the front of a word, or even both. The new words still have the same meaning and are of the same word class – so a noun remains as a noun.

■ Carry out these word subtraction sums to create some clipped words. Write down the part of the word you are removing and the word that you have created. The first one has been done for you.

■ Can you think of any words you could **clip** to invent your own new word?

hamburger – ham = burger

television – _____ = _____

refrigerator – _____ = _____

aeroplane – _____ = _____

mathematics – _____ = _____

$4 \times 9 = 36$

telephone – _____ = _____

influenza – _____ = _____

vegetable – _____ = _____

memorandum – _____ = _____

hippopotamus – _____ = _____

omnibus – _____ = _____

demonstration – _____ = _____

photograph – _____ = _____

public house – _____ = _____

examination – _____ = _____

fanatic – _____ = _____

delicatessen – _____ = _____

advertisement – _____ = _____

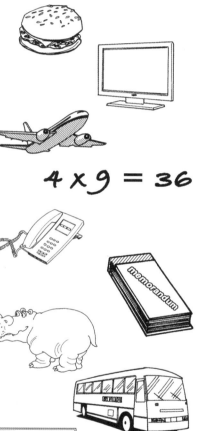

Illustrations © 2010, Catherine Ward.

Assessment

Assessment grid

The following grid shows the main objectives and activities covered in this chapter. You can use the grid to locate activities that cover a particular focus that you are keen to monitor.

Objective	Page	Activity title
To investigate the use and origins of unusual and interesting prefixes and suffixes.	36 37	Latin prefixes Greek prefixes
To use knowledge of suffix meanings to work out the definition of unfamiliar vocabulary.	38	Suffix matching game
To learn to build words from known prefixes, roots and suffixes.	40 42	Building from the roots Be afraid…be very afraid
To learn how to identify roots within words.	41	Back to the roots
To investigate words and phrases that William Shakespeare introduced into the English language.	44 45 46	Shakespearean words Double, double toil and trouble To curse or not to curse
To understand the origin of words that have been created by blending two words.	48	Portmanteau: addition word sums
To learn how words have been formed by back-formation or by shortening existing words.	49 50	Back-formation Clipping: subtraction word sums

Observation and record keeping

Maintain notes of the children who make reference to their learning from this chapter when examples are encountered and flagged up.

Assessment activity

- **What you need**
Photocopiable page 52 'Pandora's box', writing materials.
- **What to do**
Before commencing this activity, read the children the story of 'Pandora's box'. Then invite the children to use highlighters to identify 14 words in the text that contain prefixes and suffixes of Latin and Greek origin.

Differentiation

- Provide less confident learners with a number of the words, prefixes and suffixes on cards. Invite the children to match them together, reading and thinking about the word created, before finally recording those words that they are confident about.
- Challenge more confident learners to work in discussion groups with an adult, discussing the types of words they have found and created and the word class they belong to.

Further learning

- **Etymology:** Encourage the use of etymological dictionaries in class and actively encourage the children to share new vocabulary and investigate the origins of these words. Celebrate and reward children who take a proactive approach to expanding their understanding of the word roots and origins.

Name:

Assessment

Pandora's box

■ Use a highlighter to identify 20 words in this story that contain prefixes (**en-**, **re-**, **un-**, **dis-**, **de-**) and suffixes (**-ful**, **-ly**).

Zeus had been infuriated by Prometheus, who had played a cunning trick on him. In his anger, Zeus took away man's ability to make fire.

Immediately, Prometheus flew to Lemnos where a blacksmith, Hephaestus still had fire. He carried a burning torch back to man. Zeus was enraged! He swore revenge on Prometheus and began to conceive a dreadful plan.

Zeus set Hephaestus the task of creating a clay woman with a human voice. Athene, goddess of wisdom, breathed life into the clay woman. She was made beautiful by Aphrodite and was taught to deceive and be alluring by Hermes. Delighted, Zeus named this creation Pandora.

Zeus sent Pandora to Epimetheus to entrap him. Epimetheus, who had been warned never to accept gifts from Zeus, ignored Prometheus and fell in love with Pandora. They were married and for a while they lived blissfully. Now the cunning part of the trap was their wedding gift: a beautiful box that Pandora had been given by Zeus on the condition that it remained unopened.

Over time, Pandora became desperate to discover what was in the box. Eventually, she was unable to bear the suspense any longer. One day, she found herself alone. She took the hefty key and turned it in the lock and cautiously lifted the lid. Before she was able to react and slam the lid back down, the room was filled with all the evils of the world: torture, pain, disease, famine, war, violence and hatred. Pandora slammed the lid, realising what she had released.

From inside the box she heard a tiny fluttering, with nothing left to lose, she fearfully lifted the lid. As she did so, something sweet and fragile flew out. It was hope – it lingered and then disappeared out of the window.

Thereafter, the world was never the same, Zeus's plan had worked. Mortals suffered war and famine but despite all these things, they always had hope.

■ Use the roots, prefixes and suffixes to create words to describe what Pandora released and the goodness that hope can bring.

Illustrations © 2010, Catherine Ward.

Word of the week

The Word of the week pages provide information on one word linked to each section in the chapter. Each word is described in some of the following categories: word definition, word origin, word family, alternative words, fascinating facts and activities. Not all categories are relevant to every word.

You can use the words as a focus to support your work on the different sections of the chapter. For example, you could create a display around it. The information is a starting point for a word focus. The words could form part of your classroom living word bank.

You could also use the word of the week as a springboard to inspire children to think about or research fascinating facts about words, find interesting quotations and to encourage them to use dictionaries and thesauruses.

Epidemic

- **Word definition:** Noun meaning a rapid spread or increase in the occurrence of something.
- **Word origin:** From the Greek *epi-*, meaning among, and *demos*, meaning people.
- **Alternative words:** Growth, outbreak, plague, rash, scourge, spread, upsurge, wave.
- **Fascinating facts:** Joining the two Greek words *epi-* and *demos*, *epidemios* was put together to mean the spread of disease among the people. We have adapted it to become *epidemic*. *Demos* is also the root of our term *democracy*.
- **Activities:** Encourage the children to use this word in history or geography, particularly when studying the plague or other factors that affect populations of people, for example when looking into the effects of flooding and natural disasters.

Linked section:
Investigating interesting and unusual affixes, page 35

Sarcastic

- **Word definition:** An adjective meaning making scornful remarks that have or are marked by a feeling of bitterness and biting or cutting quality.
- **Word origin:** From the Greek *sarkazein*, based on *sarx* and meaning flesh.
- **Word family:** Noun: *sarcasm*.
- **Alternative words:** Acrimonious, arrogant, austere, biting, bitter, brusque, carping, caustic, contemptuous, cutting, cynical, derisive, disparaging, disrespectful, hostile, offensive, sardonic, sharp, sneering, taunting.
- **Fascinating facts:** The whole word means 'to tear flesh'. This was toned down to mean 'biting your lip' and subsequently became understood as 'making a cutting remark'. This word has similar roots to *sarcophagus*, meaning an impressive coffin, which actually meant flesh-eater.
- **Activities:** This can be used when discussing different types of humour in literacy when studying poetry. Make the links to ancient Egyptian history.

Linked section:
Dig back to the roots, page 39

Pickle

- **Word definition:** Noun meaning something preserved in brine or marinade and a troublesome or awkward situation. Verb meaning to preserve or treat in pickle.
- **Word origin:** From the Medieval German *peckel*, meaning a spicy sauce eaten with meat.
- **Alternative words:** Bind, corner, difficulty, dilemma, disorder, fix, hole, jam, predicament, quandary, scrape, tight spot.
- **Fascinating facts:** While the Medieval German *peckel* was a spicy sauce eaten with meat, *pickle* is now understood as a vegetable preserved in vinegar or other preservative. Shakespeare appears to be the first person to coin the phrase *in a pickle* to mean 'in a difficult situation', in *The Tempest*.
- **Activities:** In history, Nelson is one of the most famous people ever to have been literally 'in a pickle'. He died at the Battle of Trafalgar on 21 October 1805. He was hit by a musket ball fired from a French ship at about 1.15pm and died below decks at about 4.30pm. His body was preserved in a barrel of brandy (alcohol having pickling or preservative properties) until the ship returned home. Using this historical context, encourage the children to talk about the difference between literal and metaphorical meanings.

> **Linked section:**
> Will's words,
> page 43

Smog

- **Word definition:** Noun meaning smoke or other atmospheric pollutants combined with fog in an unhealthy or irritating mixture.
- **Word origin:** From *smoke* and *fog*, meaning smoky fog.
- **Alternative words:** Acid rain, carbon dioxide, fog, haze, smoke, soot.
- **Fascinating facts:** This is a portmanteau word, which combines *smoke* and *fog*. Its creation is attributed to Dr Henry Antoine Des Voeux who wrote about the smoky fog, which he called smog, which occurs in cities as a result of pollution. Smog used to come from burning lots of coal and the mixing of sulphur dioxide and smoke. Nowadays smog is caused by vehicle fumes that are acted on by sunlight and form a photochemical smog. It is harmful to living things.
- **Activities:** Challenge the children to research the definition of *smog*, leading into geography and PSHE, or eco-council work about pollution and environmental matters.

> **Linked section:**
> Adding and
> subtracting,
> page 47

Fun with words

Use these activities to support the vocabulary work in this chapter. They could be used as starter or plenary activities.

Cut it out
- Create a display of cuttings from magazines and newspapers of words according to their roots. For example, create a page of words of Shakespearean origin, portmanteau words or words containing Latin or Greek prefixes.

Best compliments
- Have a go at making Shakespearean compliments instead of insults – this is especially useful during February for Valentine's Day. For example, *ye sweet honey-tongued pigeon egg*.

Shakespeare's sayings
- Research and collect more of Shakespeare's expressions (*laughing stock*, *vanish into thin air*, *tower of strength*, *smells to heaven*). Ensure the children understand their meanings. Try storytelling in a circle where each child tells one part of a well-known story, such as 'Cinderella', passing an object around to signify their turn. Place the expressions on cards in the middle of the circle, and as the children retell the story they should try to incorporate the expressions into their part of the story.

Root around
- Invite the children to create a pairs game with root words (*comfort*, *hope*, *point*) and suffixes ('-ible', '-able', '-ish', '-less', '-ic', '-worthy', '-like', '-ful'). Let them choose a root card and suffix card and keep the pair if the created word is real, otherwise they should replace the cards on the table. Allow the children to word-process the cards themselves to give them ownership of the games.

Chapter 3

Grammar

Introduction

Grammar can be defined as the system of rules by which words are put together to form sentences. It is through applying grammatical rules that our language is given sense and the words we use are given meaning. Children can really enhance their writing by having a sound grammatical knowledge and a wide vocabulary. This chapter aims to enhance the children's knowledge of vocabulary that is associated with particular grammatical skills, such as placing adverbs in different positions in sentences to vary their sentence structure.

Poster notes

Parts of speech (page 57)
The poster recaps some different parts of speech: verb, adjective, adverb and conjunction. It is useful to refer to for all literacy work. You could display it in class, laminate it to use as a desk-top mat or give it to children as part of a writing skill kit to stick in their books for reference.

In this chapter

Actively adding adverbs page 58	To recognise and experiment with the positioning of adverbs in different locations in a sentence. To use adverbs to qualify verbs in writing dialogue.
Amazing adjectives page 62	To identify adjectives and understand the reason for their choice. To investigate and collect a wide range of ambitious adjectives to enhance creativity in writing.
Cooking up some verbs! page 66	To understand the importance of verb choice when using the imperative. To investigate and use powerful verbs to create descriptions.
Complex connectives page 70	To identify connectives and use more complex connectives in writing.
Assessment page 74	Activities and ideas to assess the ability to identify parts of speech in a story.

Grammar

PARTS OF SPEECH

VERB

This is a doing or being word.
Verbs can be present or past and have up to five different forms.
Verbs can be regular (**smile – smiled**) or irregular (**fly – flew**).
Modal verbs express ideas about the future (**possibility, willingness, prediction**). They include: **will, shall, can, could, must, ought, may and might.**

CONJUNCTION

This is used to link the clauses in a sentence.
They include: **and, but, so, because, although and while.**

ADJECTIVE

This is a word that describes something or somebody.
Adjectives come before a noun: **She wore an incredible hat.**
Adjectives can come after a verb: **The princess looked nervous.**
They can have comparative forms: **Mr Denton is older than Miss Simms.**
They can have superlative forms: **Miss Simms is the youngest teacher in the school.**

ADVERB

This gives extra meaning to a verb.
It can tell us how, where, when and how often.
It can show degrees of intensity and connections in meaning between sentences.
Adverbs are often formed by adding -ly to an adjective.
Many adverbs do not contain -ly, such as **outside, yesterday, never and ever.**

Illustrations © 2010, Catherine Ward.

Actively adding adverbs

Objectives

To recognise and experiment with the positioning of adverbs in different locations in a sentence. To use adverbs to qualify verbs in writing dialogue.

Background knowledge

Adverbs add to a verb. They give the reader more information and make sentences more interesting. Adverbs can come at the start of a sentence, in the middle (before a verb) or at the end. They tell us how, where, when or how often something happens. To identify an adverb you need to recognise the job it does in a sentence. Not all adverbs end in '-ly' and some words that end in '-ly' are actually adjectives. Knowing the place and role of adverbs will help to increase vocabulary.

Activities

These activities teach the children to identify adverbs, recognise the different places adverbs can go and encourage them to use adverbs to provide extra detail when writing dialogue.

● **Photocopiable page 59 'Spot the adverb'**
Use examples of adverbs from instructional texts to demonstrate how adverbs are used: *Stir the sauce rapidly*. The verb is 'stir' and the adverb tells us how to stir, so 'rapidly' is the adverb. Demonstrate how an adverb shows how often an action should take place: *Occasionally check the consistency of the sauce*. Ask the children to read the recipe on the photocopiable sheet independently and identify the adverbs in the text. Let them discuss with a talk partner which job each adverb does in the sentence. Consolidate their ideas in a plenary session.

● **Photocopiable page 60 'Using adverbs in different places'**
Explain that varying the position of adverbs adds interest. Teach the children that adverbs tell you:
  ● how something happens (*He climbed **bravely***)
  ● when or how often something happens (*He went to Cubs **regularly***) where something happens (*Tom looked **upwards** towards the sky*)
  ● to what degree something happens (*In the end, he climbed **more confidently** than all the others*).
Display this information on the board for reference. Let the children identify adverbs on the photocopiable sheet, and analyse where they were located and the role of the adverb. In the plenary session, discuss the impact of the different positions.

● **Photocopiable page 61 'Adverbs for dialogue'**
Encourage the children to use appropriate adverbs with *said* (or other dialogue words) to vary how the speaker is talking.

Further ideas

● **Getting started:** In children's independent writing, include an objective and success criteria that require children to include three sentences that start with an adverb. This will encourage them to consciously think about their use of adverbs. When they complete their writing, they should use their peers to identify the adverb starters.

What's on the CD-ROM

On the CD-ROM you will find:
● Printable versions of all three photocopiable pages.
● Answers to all three photocopiable pages.
● Interactive versions of all three photocopiable pages.

Spot the adverb

- ■ Identify and highlight the **ten** adverbs in this recipe.
- ■ Remember, to identify an adverb you need to identify the job that it does in a sentence. First find the verb and then see if there is a word that gives you more information about that verb. Is there a word that tells you how, when, how often or to what degree an action occurs?

Double chocolate American muffins
Makes 12

Ingredients
2 eggs lightly beaten
125g plain yoghurt
125ml milk
250g self-raising flour, sifted
250g caster sugar
75g cocoa powder
Pinch of salt
100g chocolate chips
Melted butter for greasing
12-hole muffin tin

Method
1. Thoroughly combine the eggs, yoghurt, coffee and milk in a large bowl.
2. Next sift together the flour, sugar, cocoa powder and salt then stir the mixture carefully.
3. Mix well.
4. Finally, stir in the chocolate chips.
5. Butter each cup of the muffin tin generously to prevent sticking.
6. Spoon in the muffin mixture almost to the top of the cups.
7. Bake in a preheated oven at 200°C for ten minutes. Reduce the temperature to 180°C and continue to bake for 15 minutes until the muffins are golden and spongy firm.
8. Serve equally between friends and family.

Illustrations © 2010, Catherine Ward.

Name:

Actively adding adverbs

Using adverbs in different places

■ Highlight the 18 adverbs in this short story.

■ Categorise where ten of the adverbs appear and what job they do in the sentence. The first one has been done for you as an example. Use another sheet of paper to complete a similar table.

Monday night was Cub night. Usually I look forward to it but this Monday was different: we were going to have a go on the abseiling wall at Scout HQ. I am totally petrified of heights and really did *not* want to go. However, my fear of being teased and taunted by Big Billy Jones was far greater so I knew I had to take a deep breath and bravely have a go!

Soon, 6 o'clock arrived. Ben's dad beeped his horn. As I got in the car, all my friends were chattering away excitedly about which Cub would climb up the most daring route on the wall. I sat quietly in the back, hoping no-one would sense my fear.

Once we arrived everyone scrambled eagerly towards our Pack Leader. "Where are your manners?" he asked jokingly. "As you're all pushing and shoving, Tom can go first. He is the only one showing any manners!"

My heart sank like a stone and suddenly I felt as if my stomach had jumped into my throat! "Come on lad, let's get you all kitted out!" Nervously, I did as I was told. All eyes were on me. Could they tell how I was actually feeling?

The next few minutes were like a blur. I went into automatic pilot mode and just did exactly as I was told. Before I knew it I was at the top of the wall. I'd done it! I'd scaled the wall and reached the top. I felt just like Sir Edmund Hillary. "Yeah! Watch out below." I called triumphantly. With a huge grin on my face, I lay back, taking the strain on the rope, and began my descent.

Adverb	Position in sentence	Role in sentence
usually	beginning	Tells you when he looked forward to it.

Illustrations © 2010, Catherine Ward.

Actively adding adverbs

Adverbs for dialogue

■ Read the story. Insert adverbs from the word bank to give the reader more information about how the words are spoken.

It was the End of Year Awards Ceremony. The children, parents, teachers and staff were all gathered in the hall. "Thank you! Thank you! Please everybody, be seated!" boomed the headteacher _____.
After a lot of bustling and scraping of chairs and further hushed whispers, everybody took their seats and looked at the stage.

"I am pleased to welcome you all to this, our annual awards ceremony, to celebrate the hard work and achievements of the past year," Mr Hopkins declared _____.

"This year we have had great success on the rugby pitches and in the swimming pool. Maybe we even have some potential Olympic athletes for the 2012 Games!" he declared _____.

"I hope he's not going to forget the netball team. We tried so hard, even though we didn't win the county tournament. I bet we don't get a mention," whispered Anna _____ to her mum.

"Be quiet and listen, just be patient, I'm sure he hasn't forgotten," Anna's Mum replied _____.

Rugby trophies, swimming certificates and football trophies were presented. "Thank you, Sir" said Alan Jones, the Year 6 Rugby Captain,

_____.

"I knew he'd forget us," hissed Anna _____.

"Finally," declared the head, "This year's Sporting Trophy of the Year for determination, hard work and a super sporting attitude, goes to the Year 5 girls' netball team!"

"There you go," whispered Mum _____.
"I told you he wouldn't forget you girls!"

"Yes!" cried Anna _____ as she held up the trophy on behalf of her team.

Word bank
sulkily   resentfully   jovially   insistently   firmly
knowingly   cheerfully   modestly   triumphantly

Amazing adjectives

To identify adjectives and understand the reason for their choice. To investigate and collect a wide range of ambitious adjectives to enhance creativity in writing.

Background knowledge

Adjectives give more information about nouns and are usually placed before the noun to provide interest and help the reader understand what is being described. Adjectives are used widely in poetry and fiction. In non-fiction they usually provide important information, such as *Cook until the cake is golden brown*.

Activities

These activities progress through identifying ambitious adjectives, to choosing and using them.

● **Photocopiable page 63 'The Great Lover'**
This extract from a poem by Rupert Brooke is essentially a descriptive list of all the things that the poet has loved in his lifetime. Invite the children to work in discussion groups to discuss the phrases and identify the adjectives in the extract. Create a class poem called 'These we have loved' and encourage the children to write about their experiences rather than people. Have a discussion before they start to help them think out their ideas.

● **Photocopiable page 64 'Sea sense'**
Each line of this poem describes the stimulation of one of the senses through the experience of being at the coast. Ask the children what they think the weather is like while the poet is writing – if the weather is stormy,

they may wish to alter verbs such as *ponder* and *stroll*. Invite the children to think of adjectives to fill the gaps, then look these up in a thesaurus to select new, more ambitious choices. For example, they might choose *sapphire* instead of *blue*.

● **Photocopiable page 65 'The dream catcher'**
Explain that dream catchers were used by American Indians to trap bad dreams. Good dreams entered through the holes in the web and the bad dreams would be shaken out in the morning. Discuss dreams that the children have had. Invite them to write adjectival phrases to describe the contents of the dream catchers. For example, there may be *an endless supply of scrumptious strawberry-flavoured chocolate drops*, or *terrorising trolls and hideous hags with warty noses*. Encourage the use of alliteration when selecting their adjectives.

Further ideas

● **Class anthology:** Each week invite two volunteers to take home an anthology of poems and select a favourite poem to write or word-process for a class anthology. They should identify descriptive vocabulary in the poem and words that they particularly like. On a specified day, invite the two volunteers to recite their poem and explain their choice and the vocabulary they particularly liked. Stick the poems into the project folder and display in the reading area. Ensure everyone has the opportunity to contribute.

 **What's on the CD-ROM**

On the CD-ROM you will find:
● Printable versions of all three photocopiable pages.
● Answers to 'The Great Lover'.

Amazing adjectives

The Great Lover

■ Read each phrase (between the semicolons) in turn. Highlight the adjectives and discuss the poet's choice of words in this part of the poem.

These I have loved:
White plates and cups, clean-gleaming,
  Ringed with blue lines; and feathery, faery dust;
    Wet roofs, beneath the lamp-light; the strong crust
    Of friendly bread; and many-tasting food;
    Rainbows; and the blue bitter smoke of wood;
  And radiant raindrops couching in cool flowers;
  And flowers themselves, that sway through sunny hours,
Dreaming of moths that drink them under the moon;
Then, the cool kindliness of sheets, that soon
Smooth away trouble; and the rough male kiss
Of blankets; grainy wood; live hair that is
Shining and free; blue-massing clouds; the keen
  Unpassioned beauty of a great machine;
  The benison* of hot water; furs to touch;
  The good smell of old clothes; and other such —
The comfortable smell of friendly fingers,
  Hair's fragrance, and the musty reek that lingers
  About dead leaves and last year's ferns…
  Dear names,
And thousand other throng to me! Royal flames;
  Sweet water's dimpling laugh from tap or spring;
  Holes in the ground; and voices that do sing;
  Voices in laughter, too; and body's pain,
  Soon turned to peace; and the deep-panting train;
Firm sands; the little dulling edge of foam
That browns and dwindles as the wave goes home;
  And washen stones, gay for an hour; the cold
  Graveness of iron; moist black earthen mould;
  Sleep; and high places; footprints in the dew;
  And oaks; and brown horse-chestnuts, glossy-new;
And new-peeled sticks; and shining pools on grass;—
    All these have been my loves.
  *blessing

by Rupert Brooke

An extract from 'The Great Lover' by Rupert Brooke; illustrations © 2010, Catherine Ward.

■ Now write a phrase to describe something that you have loved.

Name:

Amazing adjectives

Sea sense

■ Read the poem all the way through, considering why the gaps have been left.
■ Choose two adjectives to fill the gaps and use a thesaurus to look up these adjectives and find more powerful alternatives. Read your choices out loud to see which sound best before you rewrite the poem.

I stood on the cliff top gazing out across the **1** _____, **2** _____ ocean,

I clambered down to the beach to sense the **3** _____, **4** _____ sand

between my toes.

I wandered to the water's edge to eavesdrop on the conversation between the

5 _____ waves and the **6** _____ shore,

I pondered by the **7** _____ rocks and breathed in the scent of the

8 _____ seaweed,

I closed my eyes and licked my **9** _____ lips, tasting the **10** _____ flavour

of the sea.

Gap	Adjective choice 1	Adjective choice 2	Final choice
1			
2			
3			
4			
5			
6			
7			
8			
9			
10			

Amazing adjectives

The dream catcher

■ Decide whether you are going to describe a wonderful dream or a scary nightmare that has been caught by the dream catcher.

■ Create adjectival phrases to describe the contents of the dream. Use a thesaurus to help you to select really powerful adjectives. Write your adjectival phrases around the dream catcher.

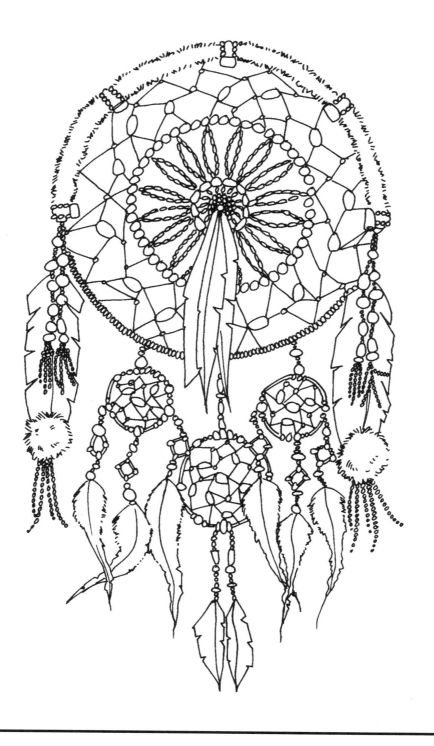

Illustrations © 2010, Catherine Ward.

Cooking up some verbs!

To understand the importance of verb choice when using the imperative. To investigate and use powerful verbs to create descriptions.

Background knowledge

Every true sentence contains a verb. Verbs express an action or a state of being and can be in the past or present tense. Modal verbs, such as *can*, *shall*, *will*, *may* and *must*, express ideas about the future. Careful choice of verbs provides their audience with a clearer picture of the action or state of being.

Activities

This section provides activities about choice of verbs, rather than form.

● **Photocopiable page 67 'Let's cook up some verbs'**
A verb in the imperative mood expresses a command, request or instruction. For example: *Come to a party!* When giving instructions it is important to choose the verbs carefully to ensure that the reader carries out the action in the correct manner. Invite the children to play a game of cookery charades to review different verbs associated with cooking. Then let them write out an imperative instruction for each picture on the photocopiable sheet.

● **Photocopiable page 68 'Every picture tells a story'**
Encourage the children to tell the story of a photograph. They should decide if they will tell the story in the first or third person. Ask them to describe who is in the photograph, where they are, what they were doing before the photograph was taken, what was happening when it was taken and what happened afterwards. Help less confident learners by carrying this out verbally first, using one of the photographs for guided writing.

● **Photocopiable page 69 'The old woman and her pig'**
Invite the children to replace the verbs with more ambitious, more interesting verbs to liven up the tale using a thesaurus to investigate synonyms for each verb. Encourage them to think about how she 'went on'. Would she get more frustrated as the story continued? How many suitable verbs can they find to replace *met* (*encountered*, *bumped into*, *chanced upon*). Encourage the children to consider how she is speaking to each character. Which verbs can they find to replace *said* (*demanded*, *ordered*, *insisted*)? Discuss the moral of the tale.

Further ideas

● **Make it better:** Find a range of simple tales (Greek myths or traditional tales, depending on what you are covering in the rest of the curriculum) that have been written for younger audiences. Ask the children to rewrite them for an older audience using more ambitious verbs.

● **Verb webs:** Create spiders' webs hanging from the ceiling with a base verb, such as *walk*, stuck in the centre on a spider. Let the children make flies with alternative verbs on to stick on to the spider's web.

What's on the CD-ROM

On the CD-ROM you will find:
● Printable versions of all three photocopiable pages.
● Answers to 'The old woman and her pig'.
● Interactive version of 'Let's cook up some verbs'.

Cooking up some verbs!

Let's cook up some verbs

■ Look at the images below. Choose a verb from the verb bank and use the imperative to write a short sentence to describe what is happening in each picture. The first one has been done for you.

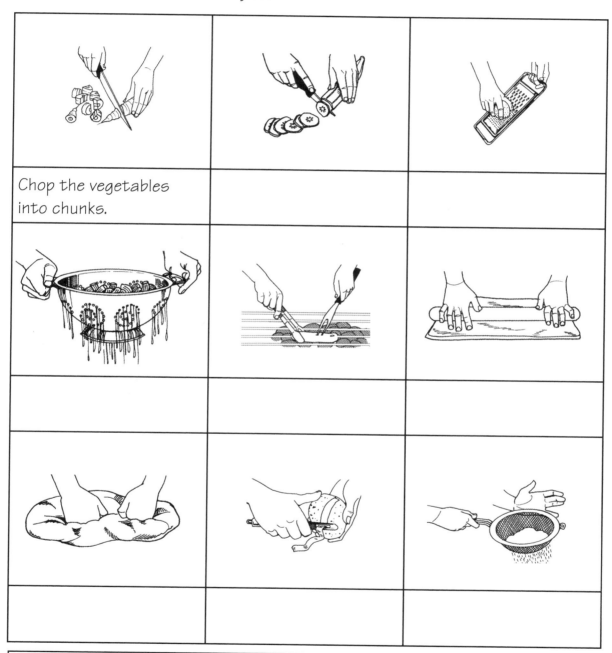

Chop the vegetables into chunks.

Verb bank

peel   chop   dice   mash   simmer   heat   bake   boil   fold   whisk
grate   grill   steam   barbecue   fry   sift   slice   blend   combine
drain   roll-out   knead   peel   squeeze   wrap   grease   roast   cover

Illustrations © 2010, Catherine Ward.

Name:

Cooking up some verbs!

Every picture tells a story

■ Choose one of the pictures below and write a story about it, using powerful verbs from the verb bank to help you. Alternatively, use a thesaurus to help you to select your own verbs.

- What do you think happened just before the picture was taken?
- What is happening at the time of the shot?
- What happened afterwards?
- Who do you think is taking the photograph and why?

Verb bank

wade
bend
balance
catch
paddle
ride
lie
plunge
leap
wait
crouch

_____

_____

_____

Verb bank

clamber
scale
ascend
hike
trek
sparkle
crunch
rumble
plummet
plunge

_____

_____

_____

_____

PHOTOCOPIABLE   **■SCHOLASTIC**
www.scholastic.co.uk

Cooking up some verbs!

The old woman and her pig
(A traditional folk tale)

■ The beginning and end of this traditional tale have been told using very dull verbs.

■ Identify all the verbs in the story and then use a thesaurus to find more powerful ones.

Beginning

Many moons ago, an old woman found a shiny penny and went to market to buy a pig. She went home with the pig walking happily by her side. On the way they came to a stile. The pig would not go over it.

So the old woman went on a bit further. She met a dog and said, "Dog! Dog! Go and bite the pig. He won't go over the stile so I won't get home tonight!" But the dog wouldn't.

So the old woman went on a bit further. She met a stick and said, "Stick! Stick! Hit the dog. The dog won't bite the pig and the pig won't go over the stile, so I won't get home tonight!" But the stick wouldn't.

End

So the old woman went on a bit further. She met a cat and said, "Cat! Cat! Scare the rat! The rat won't bite the rope. The rope won't catch the cow. The cow won't drink the water. The water won't put out the fire! The fire won't burn the stick. The stick won't hit the dog. The dog won't bite the pig and the pig won't go over the stile, so I won't get home tonight!" And the cat said "OK – if you get me a saucer of milk!"

The old woman was so surprised that she got the milk.

Then the cat scared the rat. The rat bit the rope. The rope caught the cow. The cow drank the water. The water put out the fire. The fire burnt the stick. The stick hit the dog. The dog bit the pig and the pig went over the stile. So the old woman did get home that night.

■ Write the middle part of the story in the same style using more powerful verbs and the ideas in the table.

Who she meets	What she asks them to do
Fire	Burn the stick
Water	Put out the fire
Cow	Drink the water
Rope	Catch the cow
Rat	Chew the rope

Complex connectives

Objective

To identify connectives and use more complex connectives in writing.

Background knowledge

Connectives are words or phrases that link sentences. A conjunction is a connective that links two clauses together in a sentence. A connecting adverb, phrase or clause connects ideas but the clauses remain separate. The ability to use a wide range of connectives effectively helps writers to vary their sentences and improve their writing. Connectives are used in all types of texts: in stories to show the passing of time; in persuasive texts to structure arguments (connectives of addition, opposition and reinforcement); in explanations (connectives to list, explain and indicate results).

Activities

These activities will reinforce children's understanding of the role of connectives and how and when to use them. Together with the introduction of a wider range of more ambitious connectives, the children will build their confidence and begin to use a wider range of vocabulary.

● **Photocopiable page 71 'Sorting connectives'**
The children are presented with a table of connectives, sorted according to the job they do. Discuss the meanings of the jobs and encourage the children to give their own examples for some of the connectives.

● **Photocopiable page 72 'Bravo for Brussels sprouts'**
Encourage the children to use the statements to design and create a leaflet to promote Brussels sprouts as healthy and tasty vegetables. Read the sentences together and talk about how to link sentences, compare ideas and reinforce facts. Use photocopiable page 71 'Sorting connectives' to support children. Model how to select connectives from the table and join two of the sentences: *You could boil the sprouts in salted water. Alternatively, you could stir-fry them with garlic, cream and toasted almonds.* If in season, bring in some sprouts for the children to photograph. You could even try some of the recipes and photograph the results for the leaflet.

● **Photocopiable page 73 'The perilous planet'**
This activity encourages the children to use a wide range of connectives to sequence events. Set the scene: a spacecraft, manned by scientists on a mission to collect signs of life on a newly discovered planet, has finally landed. Mission control can see the planet from its satellite and has to give directions to the astronaut scientists to get them from their landing pad to the base camp where their laboratory has been set up. Invite the children to use the list of connectives to give coherent instructions to the crew.

Further ideas

● **Out of time:** Collect connective phrases to signal time, which could be used to open sentences. For example: *As quick as a flash… Days dragged on… One miserable, murky Monday… In the blink of an eye…*

What's on the CD-ROM

On the CD-ROM you will find:
● Printable versions of all three photocopiable pages.
● Answers to 'Sorting connectives'.
● Interactive version of 'Sorting connectives'.

Complex connectives

Sorting connectives

■ The table below gives examples of different connectives and their uses.
■ For each sentence, select an appropriate connective and state the job that it is doing by writing the letter in the box.

Job	Type of connective	Examples
A	Adding information	and, also, as well as, moreover, too, furthermore
B	Sequencing ideas or events	firstly, at the start, secondly, next, meanwhile, afterwards, since, while, then, eventually, finally, in a flash, as day faded into night, whenever, instantly
C	Explaining and giving examples	although, however, for example, in other words, such as, for instance
D	Showing cause and effect	because, so, therefore, thus, consequently, if
E	Reinforcing	above all, significantly, besides, after all, especially, notably, in particular

1. I can't go to the party _____ Mum's car has broken down and we have no transport. ☐

2. The exam results improved _____ when the children used the revision packs. ☐

3. _____ the lights in the tiny cottage were turned on and glowed orange, sending out a warm friendly light into the darkness. ☐

4. The dog ate my homework diary; we had to go to Gran's house _____ I lost my pencil sharpener! ☐

5. The teacher was writing on the whiteboard _____ the children whispered among themselves. ☐

6. At the restaurant, the food was too salty when it arrived, _____ it was stone cold! ☐

7. Unfortunately, I don't like to eat green vegetables _____ I know they are good for me. ☐

Name:

Complex connectives

Bravo for Brussels sprouts

■ Use these facts about Brussels sprouts to create a leaflet to promote them as a healthy vegetable.

■ Use connectives from the table on the 'Sorting connectives' sheet and the table below to help you to argue your case.

Job	Type of connective	Examples
F	Comparing	similarly, like, as with, in the same way, equally
G	Contrasting	unlike, but, alternatively, instead, otherwise, on the other hand, however, nevertheless

- Some would say they are the UK's most hated vegetable.
- Lots of children dread the little green balls being served up on their plate.
- Many try to hide them in their mashed potato pretending they have eaten them.
- This leaflet is going to persuade you to change your mind.
- Brussels sprouts have been grown in Belgium since at least the 1200s.
- They are an excellent source of vitamin C.
- They contain lots of vitamin A.
- They are a source of folic acid and dietary fibre.
- The smell comes from sulphur released during cooking.
- Over-cooking makes the smell worse.
- Over-cooking makes the sprouts turn to mush and go slimy.
- The key is to cook them until they are just cooked and still slightly crunchy.
- You can boil the sprouts in salted water.
- You can stir-fry them with garlic, cream and toasted almonds.
- When cooked properly, Brussels sprouts have a pleasing, nutty flavour.
- Brussels sprouts should be bought on the stem. They keep longer like this.

Illustrations © 2010, Catherine Ward.

PHOTOCOPIABLE ■SCHOLASTIC
www.scholastic.co.uk

Complex connectives

The perilous planet

■ Imagine you are a space station controller. Using the map, provide a description of the route for the crew of Falcon II from their landing pad to the Space Station, Science Base I.

■ Choose from the connectives listed (or use your own connectives) to open each sentence and link your ideas.

Captain Charles spoke clearly into the radio transmitter, "This is Falcon II to Space Station Control. Do you read me?"

"Reading you loud and clear Falcon II," replied the Space Station Controller.

"We have landed and await your instructions to guide us to Science Base I," continued Captain Charles.

_____

_____

_____

_____

at the start	firstly	next	meanwhile	whenever
instantly	later	after	as soon as	eventually	finally
before	shortly	after	soon		

Illustrations © 2010, Catherine Ward.

Assessment

Assessment grid

The following grid shows the main objectives and activities covered in this chapter. You can use the grid to locate activities that cover a particular focus that you are keen to monitor.

Objective	Page	Activity title
To recognise and experiment with the positioning of adverbs in different locations in a sentence.	59 60	Spot the adverb Using adverbs in different places
To use adverbs to qualify verbs in writing dialogue.	61	Adverbs for dialogue
To identify adjectives and understand the reason for their choice.	63	The Great Lover
To investigate and collect a wide range of ambitious adjectives to enhance creativity in writing.	64 65	Sea sense The dream catcher
To understand the importance of verb choice when using the imperative.	67	Let's cook up some verbs
To investigate and use powerful verbs to create descriptions.	68 69	Every picture tells a story The old woman and her pig
To identify connectives and use more complex connectives in writing.	71 72 73	Sorting connectives Bravo for Brussels sprouts The perilous planet

Observation and record keeping

Encourage the children to self-assess their written work. Can they highlight where they have used connectives? Have they varied their sentence openers? Remind the children regularly to try to include sentences that start with adverbs or '-ing' words.

Assessment activity

- **What you need**
Photocopiable page 75 'Greyfriars Bobby', writing implements, coloured pencils or highlighters.
- **What to do**
The photocopiable sheet provides a short, simple recount of the historical story of Greyfriars Bobby. Children should read the story through entirely. Then ask them to use four different coloured markers to highlight examples of each of the four main parts of speech. The examples they find should be recorded in the table provided.

Differentiation

- Less confident learners may carry out this assessment as a group reading discussion to reinforce their understanding of parts of speech.
- More confident learners may go on to find areas of the text where they think they could replace verbs or add adjectives to increase the effectiveness of the text.

Further learning

- **Adverbial phrases:** Extend work on adverbs to explain what is meant by adverbial phrases. Scan books for useful examples.
- **Subjects:** Encourage the children to consider vocabulary choices in all subject areas. For example, when writing up investigations in science, explain that they will be using the imperative and encourage careful choice of verbs. In history, when recounting famous events, encourage the use of ambitious connectives to sequence events. Make links to literacy whenever possible to enable the children to see how their learning is put into practice.

Assessment

Greyfriars Bobby

■ Read this recount. Use four different-coloured pencils or highlighters to highlight at least **five** nouns, **five** powerful verbs, **five** adjectives and **five** adverbs.

■ Create a key at the bottom. Compare your findings with a talk partner.

In the early 1800s, John Gray, a gardener, his wife Jess and son John came to Edinburgh to find work. However, that winter the weather was harsh. Consequently, unable to find work as a gardener, he joined the Edinburgh Police Force.

To accompany him in his role as a night watchman, John took on a partner, a small Skye Terrier who he named Bobby. Together John and Bobby became faithful friends. Relentlessly, they trudged through the old, cobbled streets of Edinburgh on their watch. On the 8th February 1858 John sadly died of tuberculosis, a horrible disease of the lungs. He was buried in Greyfriars Churchyard.

This is where the story really begins. Bobby deeply missed his master and refused to leave his master's grave. Through howling winds and torrential rain, Bobby remained at his grave. The gardener tried on numerous occasions to evict Bobby from the churchyard. Eventually, he conceded defeat and built a shelter for Bobby by placing sacking at the side of John Gray's grave, beneath two stones.

Every day, at 1 o'clock, the time-gun that boomed out from Edinburgh Castle signalled to Bobby that it was time to leave for his daily meal. Bobby followed William Dow, a local cabinet-maker to the same Coffee House where he used to go with his master. Here, each day, he was given a meal.

A bye-law was passed some years later that decreed that any dog without a licence would be destroyed. As Bobby no longer had a master, it would seem that his fate was sealed. Fortunately, Bobby's determined dedication and loyalty to his dead master had made him famous. Sir William Chambers decided to pay Bobby's licence. The little dog was presented with a collar with a brass inscription. For fourteen long years, the dead man's faithful little dog maintained a constant watch over his master's grave, only leaving to eat.

In 1873, a granite fountain with a statue of Bobby placed on top was erected by the Edinburgh City Council in memory of the incredible little dog. Bobby's headstone reads, 'Greyfriars Bobby – died 14th January 1872 – aged 16 years – Let his loyalty and devotion be a lesson to us all.'

Part of speech	Colour	Part of speech	Colour
Noun		Adjective	
Powerful verb		Adverb	

Word of the week

The Word of the week pages provide information on one word linked to each section in the chapter. Each word is described in some of the following categories: word definition, word origin, word family, alternative words, fascinating facts and activities. Not all categories are relevant to every word.

You can use the words as a focus to support your work on the different sections of the chapter. For example, you could create a display around it. The information is a starting point for a word focus. The words could form part of your classroom living word bank.

You could also use the word of the week as a springboard to inspire children to think about or research fascinating facts about words, find interesting quotations and to encourage them to use dictionaries and thesauruses.

Shrewdly

- **Word definition:** An adverb meaning astute or sharp in practical matters.
- **Word origin:** From Middle English *shrew* meaning wicked.
- **Word family:** Adjective: *shrewd*; noun: *shrew*.
- **Alternative words:** Acutely, artfully, astutely, cagily, cannily, cunningly, cuttingly, discerningly, judiciously, keenly, knowingly, perceptively, piercingly, profoundly, prudently, sensibly, slyly, smartly, wisely.
- **Fascinating facts:** If you carry out an action shrewdly it means that you have made a clever judgement. However, in the 14th century it actually meant something totally different. It meant wicked. This came from the noun *shrew*, meaning a wicked man. Shakespeare used the term in *The Taming of the Shrew*, the shrew referring to a bad-tempered old woman.
- **Activities:** Invite the children to use the adverb in peer assessment to decide how tasks have been carried out.

Linked section: Actively adding adverbs, page 58

Groggy

- **Word definition:** An adjective meaning staggering, as from exhaustion or blows and dazed and weakened, as from lack of sleep.
- **Alternative words:** Befuddled, confused, dazed, dopey, drunken, faint, hazy, out of it, punch-drunk, punchy, reeling, shaky, slaphappy, staggering, stupefied, swaying, tired, unsteady, weak, whirling, wobbly, woozy.
- **Fascinating facts:** Grog originally referred to a mix of rum and water, which sailors in the Royal Navy were given on a daily basis. Admiral Edward Vernon introduced this activity in 1740 to stop the sailors from getting really drunk by drinking neat rum. He always wore a coat made of grogram, a coarse cloth, and was nicknamed Old Grogram, from this association came the term *grog*. Sailors who drank too much grog, had hangover symptoms and were described as groggy.

Linked section: Amazing adjectives, page 62

Hector

● **Word definition:** A verb meaning to domineer or drive into compliance by the use of as threats or force, for example.
● **Word origin:** From the Greek, *Hektor*.
● **Alternative words:** Bludgeon, browbeat, bulldoze, bully, bullyrag, cow, menace, threaten.
● **Fascinating facts:** Hector was a Trojan warrior in Greek mythology so the word was originally associated with a hero. Later it changed to referring to a bully.
● **Activities:** This word can be used in PSHE as a route to discussing bullying. Encourage the children to research characters in history who hectored people and were famous bullies.

Linked section: Cooking up some verbs!, page 66

But

● **Word definition:** A connective indicating contrast.
● **Word origin:** From the Old English *butan*, meaning outside.
● **Alternative words:** However, on the other hand, nevertheless, still, yet, though, although.
● **Fascinating facts:** While this connective originally came from *butan*, meaning outside, it evolved to mean without or except, and has been used since the 12th century.

Linked section: Complex connectives, page 70

Fun with words

∙∙∙

Use these activities to support the vocabulary work in this chapter. They could be used as starter or plenary activities.

Sentence starters
● Children will need whiteboards and pens. At the start of the lesson, hold up a sentence starter for the children to use to create a sentence. Each week choose a different daily theme to reinforce the different ways of opening sentences. For example, one week, begin with adverbs (*delightedly*, *quietly*, *suddenly*, *surprisingly* or *apologetically*). The second week you could begin with a simile (*moving as slowly as a tortoise* or *smiling like a Cheshire cat*). The third week you could provide verbs in the present continuous form to start with (*laughing*, *scowling*, *mumbling*, *sighing*, *panting*) and so on.

Connective caller
● Invite the children to sit in a circle and create a story by supplying one sentence each – the funnier, the better. The 'connective caller' uses a selection of connectives on cards in between each sentence to direct the way the story goes. For example, start with the simple sentence: *One day Milly decided to go shopping*. The connective caller may decide to hold up *however*. The second child responds: *All the buses were full*. The story continues for a set period or until it reaches a natural conclusion.

Definition game
● Fill a bag with cards, each containing a different noun (from *banana* to *beanbag*). Split the class into two teams with a 'describer' on each. The aim of the game is for the team to correctly guess as many of the words described as possible within a set time. Use an egg timer for each session. The describer holds the bag and draws out a card on the signal to go. They continue describing the object until someone in their team calls out the correct noun. They then pick another card and begin describing that. They continue until the session ends. The winning team is the one with the most correct guesses.

The sentence doctor
● If possible, bring in a stethoscope and white laboratory coat for this activity. Write a simple sentence with no punctuation or capital letters. Explain that you are in need of a 'sentence doctor' to treat this rather sick sentence. The sentence doctor should wear the white coat and stethoscope and 'operate' on the sentence. They may call on the help of 'nurses' and 'theatre staff' if necessary. Begin by correcting the sentence and then add in new words, change words and begin to build the sentence into a more complex sentence with ambitious vocabulary. For example, *The dog bit the cat* may become *Without warning, the rabid, slavering hound pounced on the defenceless feline, who was lazing innocently in the afternoon sun, and sunk his razor-sharp canines into her flesh.*

Chapter 4

Cross-curricular vocabulary

Introduction

Children encounter a wide range of technical vocabulary across the curriculum. This chapter provides the opportunity for consolidating and refreshing children's understanding of some of the vocabulary which they will have encountered by and during Year 5.

Poster notes

Connectives (page 80)

The poster provides examples of the different functions of connectives and examples of each type. In science, connectives that link ideas relating to cause and effect will be particularly useful in writing conclusions to investigations. In history, connectives that help to sequence events will be useful when recounting. In geography, connectives that explain ideas and give examples will be of particular use – for example, when describing the formation of river features. In maths, sequencing connectives can be useful when explaining a mathematical process. Encourage the children to think about the different classes of connectives and to relate them to work they have carried out and where they may use them.

In this chapter

Making sense of science page 81	To consolidate understanding of a range of scientific vocabulary. To consolidate specific science vocabulary.
A world of words page 85	To consolidate a range of geographical vocabulary. To use geographical vocabulary in group discussions.
Mastering maths talk page 89	To consolidate and use mathematical vocabulary.
Defining the past page 93	To use vocabulary associated with developing chronological awareness. To consolidate and use a range of historical vocabulary.
Assessment page 97	Activities and ideas to assess use of the more complex connectives outlined on the poster.

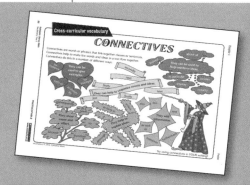

Cross-curricular vocabulary

CONNECTIVES

Connectives are words or phrases that link together clauses or sentences.
Connectives help to make the words and ideas in a text flow together.
Connectives do this in a number of different ways:

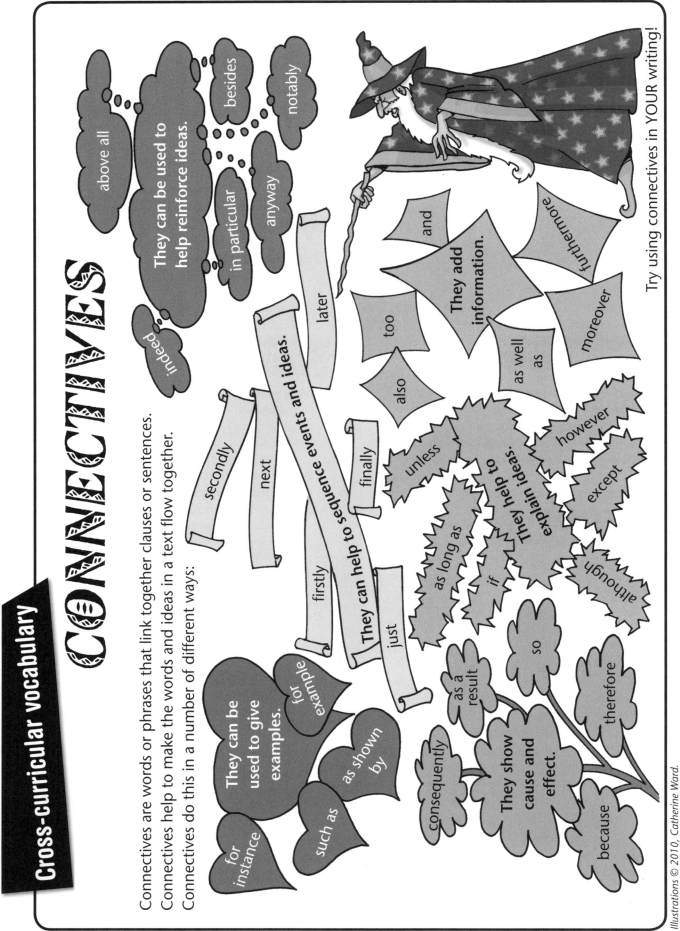

above all

They can be used to help reinforce ideas.

besides

notably

in particular

anyway

indeed

and

They add information.

furthermore

too

also

as well as

moreover

later

secondly

next

They can help to sequence events and ideas.

firstly

finally

just

unless

as long as

if

They help to explain ideas.

however

except

although

so

as a result

therefore

consequently

They show cause and effect.

because

They can be used to give examples.

for example

for instance

such as

as shown by

Try using connectives in YOUR writing!

Illustrations © 2010, Catherine Ward.

Making sense of science

Objectives

To consolidate understanding of a range of scientific vocabulary. To consolidate specific science vocabulary.

Background knowledge

The teaching of Attainment Target 1 in science involves using technical vocabulary, which will be used and built on throughout Key Stages 1 and 2. It is important that the children develop a sound understanding of the definitions of these words and develop the confidence to use them freely.

Activities

A bank of scientific vocabulary, particularly vocabulary associated with investigative work, which is progressively introduced through Key Stages 1 and 2 can be built upon and reinforced. However, where there is not a progressive introduction and reinforcement of terms, children will need to be introduced to them. These activities cover the vocabulary that is expected to be learned by and during Year 5.

● **Photocopiable page 82 'Science investigations'**
Science investigations form the backbone of learning in science throughout the Key Stage 1 and 2 curriculum. As the children progress through the Key Stages the vocabulary associated with investigations also becomes more complex. This activity consolidates and reinforces understanding of the terms involved in the different levels of an upper Key Stage 2 investigation.

● **Photocopiable pages 83 and 84 'Vocabulary trail game'**
Invite the children to work in groups of five (two in each team with a quiz master) to play a science-based vocabulary game. Each team needs about ten coloured counters (red for team A and blue for team B, for example), one game board (an enlarged copy of the photocopiable sheet) and a copy of the question sheet for the quiz master. Decide who is to be in team A and who is to be in team B. The aim of the game is to cover a line of tiles travelling from left to right. The opposing team have to try to block the route by answering questions correctly and covering tiles with their counters. Each question is derived from the Key Stage 2 science Programme of Study and requires answers that start with the letters on the tile in question. The vocabulary chosen represents terms that the children will need to know by the end of Key Stage 2.

Further ideas

● **Quiz busters:** An online version of the science trail game, called 'Quiz Busters', can be found at www.teachers-direct.co.uk. The resource is ideal for using in plenary sessions in any subject.
● **Quiz:** Children can draw on their own knowledge and create their own quizzes to try out on their peers using the above link. This is an excellent way to introduce and reinforce subject-specific vocabulary and to reinforce the skill of asking questions.

 **What's on the CD-ROM**

On the CD-ROM you will find:
● Printable versions of all three photocopiable pages.
● Answers to 'Science investigations'.
● Interactive versions of 'Science investigations' and 'Vocabulary trail game'.

Name:

Making sense of science

Science investigations

■ Use the words in the word bank below to complete the gaps, showing you understand the vocabulary of investigations.

Stage 1: What am I investigating? First of all you need to think of a

_____ for your investigation.

Stage 2: What do I think is going to happen? Next you need to make a

_____ to say what you think will happen in your investigation.

Stage 3: Why do I think this will happen? Now you need to form a

_____ and say why you think your _____ is correct.

Stage 4: What will I change? Then you need to think about the one thing you

are going to change – this is called the _____.

Stage 5: What will I keep the same? You need to keep everything else the same

so that you are doing a _____ test.

Stage 6: What will I observe? Next you will have to decide what you are going

to be _____.

Stage 7: How will I record what I find? You will need to record your

_____ in a table or on a graph.

Stage 8: Describing what happened. After the investigation you will need to see

if your results followed a _____. You will also need to see if any of

the results did not fit into the _____ and explain why.

Stage 9: What does your investigation tell you? Finally, you need

to make a _____. You need to say if your results were

what you _____ and then you need to explain why your

_____ was right or wrong. This will help you to say what you have

discovered from your investigation.

question	prediction	prediction	pattern	hypothesis
variable	recording	fair	pattern	results
conclusion	predicted	hypothesis		

Making sense of science

Vocabulary trail game (1)

■ You need: a question master and two teams; ten coloured counters for each team.

■ The aim is to complete a trail from left to right by answering questions correctly. The answer to the question begins with the letter on the selected tile.

■ If a team answers a question correctly, they place one of their coloured counters on that tile. The other team can then choose a tile and answer the question for it. The idea of the game is to block the other team's trail and make your own way across the board. Good luck!

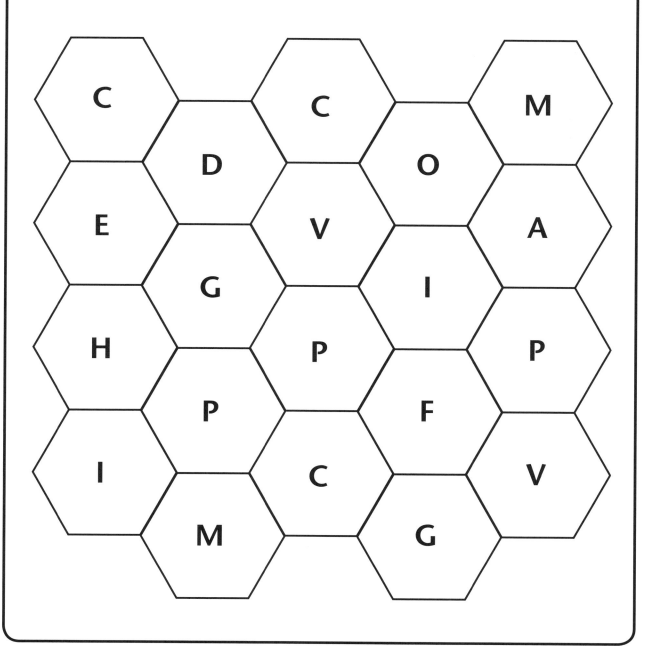

Name:

Making sense of science

Vocabulary trail game (2)

■ If you are the question master, keep this sheet hidden from the players.
■ When a letter is chosen by a player, read the corresponding question and check their answer against the answers on the sheet.

What **C** is when water cools and changes from water vapour to water? **CONDENSATION**	What **D** is an example of a reversible change? **DISSOLVING**	What **C** are used for tearing and ripping food? **CANINES**	What **O** is a material that does not let light through? **OPAQUE**	What **M** is measured in g or kg and is a measure of how much matter something contains? **MASS**
What **E** is when a liquid changes into a gas? **EVAPORATION**	What **G** is when a seed starts to grow? **GERMINATION**	What **V** is the name for animals with backbones? **VERTEBRATES**	What **I** describes materials that do not allow heat to travel through them? **INSULATORS**	What **A** is the imaginary line through the Earth on which it rotates? **AXIS**
What **H** is lighter than air? **HELIUM**	What **P** is the process by which plants make food? **PHOTOSYNTHESIS**	What **P** is the name for plants because they make their own food? **PRODUCERS**	What **F** is a force between two surfaces that are sliding across one another? **FRICTION**	What **P** describes rocks like sandstone, which let water through them? **PERMEABLE**
What **I** describes a change that cannot be undone, like frying an egg? **IRREVERSIBLE**	What **M** are viruses, bacteria and fungi all types of? **MICRO-ORGANISMS**	What **C** is the name for animals, because they eat other plants and animals? **CONSUMERS**	What **G** is the force that makes things fall back to Earth? **GRAVITY**	What **V** describes what makes sounds? **VIBRATIONS**

A world of words

Objectives

To consolidate a range of geographical vocabulary.
To use geographical vocabulary in group discussions.

Background knowledge

Children may have learned many geographical terms but feel unable to use them confidently. This section provides a glossary of terms related to rivers and coasts and vocabulary linked to environmental issues affecting our planet today from upper Key Stage 2. Speaking and listening group activities will encourage the children to begin using this vocabulary.

Activities

These activities help to develop geographical vocabulary for use in real situations.

● **Photocopiable page 86 'Rivers and coasts glossary'**
This glossary includes general geographical terms for upper Key Stage 2 geography. Children should match the terms to their definitions in alphabetical order. Discuss the vocabulary in terms of topics that have been covered, words they have encountered outside school and new terms. Ensure the children have an understanding of all the vocabulary as it will be used in the subsequent activities.

● **Photocopiable page 87 'Climate talk'**
Use this as a teaching tool to introduce the most common vocabulary related to current environmental issues. Discuss the terms as the children complete the climate talk glossary in preparation for group discussion activities. Prepare an image slideshow to accompany each definition.

● **Photocopiable page 88 'Geography debate cards'**
This photocopiable sheet provides statements relating to current environmental issues, including climate change and flooding. Divide the class into six groups of five and allocate each member of each group a different coloured sticker. Call these the rainbow groups. Choose one card for the session and give each group a copy of it. Tell the groups to discuss the issue and state their opinions and ideas, using as many examples of the new vocabulary as possible. After a specified time, split the groups to form single colour groups (all the reds, all the blues, and so on). Each new group should share the ideas from their rainbow group. The colours then return to their original rainbow groups to feed back any new information they have gathered. Each group then puts forward a presentation of the collaborative ideas and views discussed. Encourage the children to use the connectives on the poster, too. For every word included from the glossary, award ten points to the class. Repeat the discussion group process with a different statement card on a different occasion. Record the vocabulary points awarded and see which debate encouraged the best use of geographical vocabulary.

Further ideas

● **News round:** Go to the CBBC Newsround website and print off articles about flooding, natural disasters and other geographical issues that hit the headlines. Display on a class news board. Encourage the children to give their views, encouraging the use of geographical vocabulary. Invite them to word-process speech bubble quotes of their views.

What's on the CD-ROM

On the CD-ROM you will find:
● Printable versions of all three photocopiable pages.
● Answers to 'Rivers and coasts glossary' and 'Climate talk'.
● Interactive versions of 'Rivers and coasts glossary' and 'Climate talk'.

Name:

A world of words

Rivers and coasts glossary

■ Cut out the cards and match the words to their definitions.

An area of deposition found at the mouth of the river – triangular in shape.	This is formed when the roof of an arch collapses and leaves a steep tower of rock in the sea.	Where two rivers meet.
A wooden or stone-built structure that sticks out into the sea to stop sand being washed away.	These are where a river flows very rapidly and the water foams and looks white.	The rise and fall of the sea twice a day.
This is formed when waves erode a cave until water flows completely through a headland.	A bend in the river – usually in the middle or lower course	Created by the wind blowing over the surface of the sea.
The dropping or depositing of river-borne material.	The wearing away of rock and soil found along the river bed and banks.	Small rivers or streams that flow into a larger river.
tributaries	deposition	erosion
arch	rapids	groyne
waves	confluence	stack
delta	tide	meander

A world of words

Climate talk

■ Write the correct word next to its definition.

Vocabulary	Definition
	This is the increase in the world's temperature caused in part by the greenhouse effect.
	Trees are cut down to clear land for farming and building or to use the wood for building or fuel. If they are not replanted the forests will shrink. The removal of the trees means forest habitats are destroyed.
	This is an extended period of extremely dry weather.
	Coal, natural gas and petrol are examples of these. They contain carbon and are made of the remains of prehistoric plants and animals. They take millions of years to form and produce carbon dioxide when burned.
	This is the envelope of gases that surrounds the Earth. The gases are held there by gravity.
	An invisible layer of gases in our atmosphere allows heat from the sun through but absorbs some of the heat coming back from the Earth's surface. Certain gases act like a blanket and keep the surface of the Earth warm. Burning fossil fuels releases large amounts of carbon dioxide into the atmosphere. This disrupts the natural balance of the Earth's climate, causing climate change.
	This happens when changes to the environment and the climate can make conditions unsuitable for certain species to survive.
	This occurs when a river bursts its banks and the water spills on to the flood plain. It can be worse in urban areas because they have large amounts of concrete that prevents water from seeping into the ground.
	These are rivers of compacted ice formed over long periods of time, which move very slowly. Global warming is causing them to melt and the extra water is making sea levels rise.

atmosphere   deforestation   droughts   flooding   fossil fuels
glaciers   extinction   greenhouse effect   global warming

Name:

A world of words

Geography debate cards

■ In your groups, use the card selected for debate and make notes on the ideas that you share.

✂

Energy use What do you need energy for? How could we cut down our energy consumption in the home, at school or work, and in the streets? What alternatives could governments, companies and individuals use instead of fossil fuels?	**Deforestation** What effects do you think deforestation has on wildlife? What effects do you think it has on the local economy? How could local people make a living if they do not have money as a result of deforestation? What effect does deforestation have on the amount of carbon dioxide in the atmosphere?
Food miles How far do you think a banana has travelled from where it grew to get into your stomach? What would it mean if we did not have food from abroad? How could we produce more food locally?	**Endangered animals** We are the only species on Earth that is causing damage to the environment. What actions do you think you do that have an impact on the survival of species like the polar bear? What can you do to help stop these extinctions?
Flooding Why is flooding becoming so much more common? What impact does it have on people's lives?	**Fossil fuels** Talk about all the uses you can think of for petrol, oil, coal and gas. What do you think would happen if we ran out of fossil fuels? What could we use instead?

PHOTOCOPIABLE   ■SCHOLASTIC
www.scholastic.co.uk

Mastering maths talk

Objective

To consolidate and use mathematical vocabulary.

Background knowledge

Children cannot learn the meanings of new vocabulary in isolation. All vocabulary needs to be learned in a real context through oral practice, particularly through using questioning. To understand mathematical ideas requires a sound understanding of the vocabulary involved and this will be learned through repeated use in a variety of different ways to ensure ambiguities are ironed out. The vocabulary children will encounter by and in Year 5 is detailed in the National Numeracy Strategy *Mathematical Vocabulary Book*.

Activities

The activities in this section provide ideas for oral practice using mathematical vocabulary that may be used in everyday language.

● **Photocopiable page 90 'The detective and the digit dilemma'**

Invite the children to act as detectives to solve a 'digit dilemma'. Using statements that incorporate mathematical vocabulary, encourage the children to work out the identity of the mystery number. Ask them to tell you how many stages they needed to go through before they had sufficient evidence to identify the number. Challenge them to work in pairs to create their own digit dilemmas. Award points for each different term used. Which pair can use the most terms before the detective identifies the number? This concept could be extended to include fractions, 2D or 3D shapes, times of the day and so on.

● **Photocopiable page 91 'Explain yourself!'**

This activity encourages children to verbalise how they would approach a multi-layered mathematical dilemma involving different aspects of maths. The open questions are designed to draw out mathematical vocabulary. The questions are generic and may be applied to any word problem that the children are presented with. Use the possible answers to lead the children who find it difficult to verbalise their methods.

● **Photocopiable page 92 'Maths trail game'**

Challenge the children to work in groups of five (two in each team with a quiz master) to play a maths vocabulary quiz. Each team needs about ten coloured counters (red for team A and blue for team B, for example), one game board (Use the game board from photocopiable page 83 'Science trail game (1)') and a copy of the question sheet for the quiz master. Decide who is to be in team A and who is to be in team B. The aim of the game is to cover a line of tiles travelling from left to right. The opposing team have to try to block the route by answering questions correctly and covering tiles with their counters.

Further ideas

● **Play maths:** Provide regular opportunities for the children to play maths board games, solve maths puzzles and do maths quizzes in a wide range of mathematical contexts. Encourage the children to explain how they solved the problems, drawing out the target vocabulary.

 What's on the CD-ROM

On the CD-ROM you will find:
● Printable versions of all three photocopiable pages.
● Answers to 'The detective and the digit dilemma' and 'Explain yourself!'.

Name:

Mastering maths talk

The detective and the digit dilemma

■ This digit dilemma uses ten different mathematical terms (in bold). Use your maths detective skills to work out what I am.

I am a three **digit** number.
I am an **odd** number.
I am **divisible** by 5.
I am a **multiple** of 3.
My digits **total** 9.
All of my digits are **different**.
All of my digits are odd.
The **hundreds** digit is **greater than** the **tens** digit.
I am **less than** 400.
What number am I? _____

■ Work in pairs to create your own digit dilemmas using as many different vocabulary terms as possible.
■ First choose a number for your dilemma. Then begin writing your statements for the detective to use to puzzle out what your number is. How many stages does the detective need to go through until they are sure of the answer?
■ You score ten points for each different mathematical term used in your digit dilemma.

digit	double	greater than	less than	total	multiple	factor
halve	odd	even	divisible	square	hundreds	prime	total
decrease	increase	consecutive	square root	difference	subtract

Illustrations © 2010, Catherine Ward.

Mastering maths talk

Explain yourself!

- ■ Draw a triangle where the size of each angle is a square number.
- ■ Use the questions below to prepare a talk about your triangle and how you constructed it.

1. What facts do you know about triangles and square numbers already?

2. What do you need to find out or do in order to work out the angles if they are to be square numbers?

3. What operations are you going to use?

4. What equipment will you need to draw your triangle?

5. Draw your triangle on the back of the sheet. How did you construct it?

6. What facts can you tell me about your triangle?

Name:

Mastering maths talk

Maths trail game

- If you are the question master, keep this sheet hidden from the players.
- When a letter is chosen by a player, read the corresponding question and check their answer against the answers on the sheet.

What I is another name for a whole number? **INTEGER**	What H describes the x-axis on a graph? **HORIZONTAL**	What E is a good guess? **ESTIMATE**	What C is the amount of liquid a container will hold when it is full? **CAPACITY**
What M is an average found by adding all the numbers and dividing by how many numbers there are? **MEAN**	What P describes two lines drawn at right angles to each other? **PERPENDICULAR**	What G is an imperial measure of capacity equal to 8 pints or 4.546 litres? **GALLON**	What D is the distance straight across a circle, passing through the centre? **DIAMETER**
What C is the distance around a circle? **CIRCUMFERENCE**	What P describes two lines that are always the same distance apart and will therefore never meet? **PARALLEL**	What V is a line that is standing straight up and is at right angles to the Earth's surface? **VERTICAL**	What C refers to numbers that are next to each other in a sequence? **CONSECUTIVE**
What G is a diagram used to show the relationship between two or more variable quantities? **GRAPH**	What F is an expression using letters showing how to calculate one quantity in terms of another? **FORMULA**	What I describes a fraction whose numerator is greater than its denominator? **IMPROPER**	What O is an eight-sided polygon? **OCTAGON**
What V describes a type of diagram for sorting data? **VENN**	What P describes a shape with three or more sides? **POLYGON**	What A is the name of an angle less than 90°? **ACUTE**	What M is produced by timesing a starting number by another whole number? **MULTIPLE**

■SCHOLASTIC
www.scholastic.co.uk

Defining the past

Objectives

To use vocabulary associated with developing chronological awareness. To consolidate and use a range of historical vocabulary.

Background knowledge

'Chronology provides a mental framework or map which gives significance and coherence to the study of history.' (*Final Report of the History National Curriculum Working Group*, 1990.) There are many ways of expressing periods of time, which will be grasped as children's understanding of past events matures. Likewise, the teaching of vocabulary associated with time is not simply about understanding the meaning of a word, but using it in a historical context as a tool to describe and place events.

Activities

This section provides activities to help develop children's appreciation of the vocabulary associated with chronology to provide them with the tools to help develop historical understanding.

● **Photocopiable page 94 'Sorting time'**
This provides a stimulus for using vocabulary terms associated with chronology. Encourage the children to organise time terms and discuss what events may occur for each duration. For example, a second – the blink of an eye. Explain the origins of the terms AD and BC. Explain what is meant by the Common Era and point out that not everyone uses the Christian Western system of chronology. Let the children allocate AD or BC to the vocabulary terms to stimulate group or whole-class discussions about time periods. Note how well children use terms such as *ancient*, *medieval*, *modern*, *long ago* and *recent*. Create a bank of time words on the whiteboard.

● **Photocopiable page 95 'Chronology of British history'**
This sets out the main periods in British history. Invite the children to work in pairs to insert the events into the correct time period. Discuss the duration of each of these periods, how long ago events occurred and how long there was between these events. Use the vocabulary of time to discuss the events in relation to each other. Encourage the children to use *decades*, *centuries*, *millennia*, *approximately* and *between*. The highlighted words represent vocabulary that may need clarification.

● **Photocopiable page 96 'Top history terms'**
Invite children to find the meanings of the historical terms using dictionaries or online sites, such as www.historyonthenet.com. As a homework exercise, ask the children to carry out further research in order to write a sentence containing the word in a real historical context. Pool the results and order them chronologically and geographically.

Further ideas

● **Web glossary:** At the beginning of the year set up class glossaries for each subject on the class page of the school website. Encourage the children to add new terms as they encounter them, rewarding effort. Challenge the class to insert a set number of terms for each subject.

What's on the CD-ROM

On the CD-ROM you will find:
● Printable versions of all three photocopiable pages.
● Answers to 'Sorting time'.
● Interactive versions of all three photocopiable pages.

Name:

Defining the past

Sorting time

■ The words in the box are all used to describe time periods.

■ Starting with the term that denotes the shortest period of time, put them in order and describe an event that takes each different amount of time.

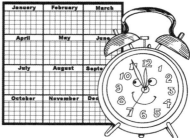

| hour   year   century   day |
| minute   millennium   week   second |
| decade   month |

Time period	An event that lasts for this duration

Dionysius Exiguus, a Christian monk and scholar, was asked by the Pope to work out when Jesus was born in order to develop a calendar so that events in history could all be related to whether they occurred before or after the birth of Jesus Christ. Christendom adopted the calendar in the 6th century AD (525) so that dates became referred to as occurring AD (Anno Domini: meaning in the year of the Lord) or BC (Before Christ: meaning before the birth of Jesus Christ).

It is thought that Dionysius miscalculated the year of Jesus' birth and that Jesus was actually born four years earlier. Dionysius also omitted to count the first year of Jesus' life in his calculations (from his birth to his first birthday).

■ If we correct Dionysius' calculations, what would your year of birth actually be and what should we call this year?

Illustrations © 2010, Catherine Ward.

Defining the past

Chronology of British history

■ Can you work out which period in history these key events happened in? Check that you know the meaning of the highlighted words. Create a timeline on another sheet of paper.

Time period	Dates	Time period	Dates
Neolithic and Bronze Age	8000–800 BC	Tudors	AD 1485–1603
Iron Age	800 BC–AD 43	Civil war and revolution	AD 1603–1714
Roman Empire	AD 43–410	British Empire and sea power	AD 1714–1837
Viking and Anglo Saxon invasions	AD 410–1066	Victorian Britain	AD 1837–1901
Norman Britain	AD 1066–1154	World Wars	AD 1901–1945
Middle Ages	AD 1154–1485	Modern Britain	AD 1945–now

Key events in British history

● 6000 BC – Britain finally separates from mainland Europe.

● AD 2003 – Britain joins an **invasion** of Iraq.

● AD 793 – Vikings attack the **monastery** at Lindisfarne.

● AD 1066 – Edward the Confessor is killed and Harold becomes King of England.

● AD 1085 – **Domesday Book** is put together to **survey** England's land and people.

● AD 1945 – Britain celebrates the end of War in Europe (**VE Day**).

● AD 1337 – Hundred Years War begins between England and France.

● AD 1477 – William Caxton invents the printing press.

● AD 1914 – Archduke Franz Ferdinand is **assassinated**. World War I begins.

● AD 597 – Augustine arrives in England and begins its **conversion** to Christianity.

● AD 122 – Emperor Hadrian orders **construction** of a wall across northern Britain.

● AD 1605 – The Gunpowder Plot to assassinate James I is discovered.

● AD 1965 – The death penalty is **abolished**.

● AD 43 – Roman Emperor Claudius orders the invasion of Britain.

● AD 1653 – Oliver Cromwell makes himself **Lord Protector**.

● AD 1771 – Britain's first cotton **mill** is opened.

● AD 1837 – Victoria comes to the throne after William IV dies.

● AD 1558 – Elizabeth I accedes to the throne.

Name:

Defining the past

Top history terms

■ Use a dictionary or encyclopedia to find the meaning of this historical vocabulary.

■ Then on another sheet of paper write a sentence using each word.

Vocabulary	Definition
accession	To take up an important position, usually the throne.
allies	
aristocracy	
civil war	
depose	
exile	
government	
imperialism	
industrialisation	
invasion	
occupation	
parliament	
pioneer	
revolution	
treaty	
tyrant	

PHOTOCOPIABLE ■ SCHOLASTIC
www.scholastic.co.uk

Assessment

Assessment grid

The following grid shows the main objectives and activities covered in this chapter. You can use the grid to locate activities that cover a particular focus that you are keen to monitor.

Objective	Page	Activity title
To consolidate understanding of a range of scientific vocabulary.	82	Science investigations
To consolidate specific science vocabulary.	83 84	Vocabulary trail game (1) Vocabulary trail game (2)
To consolidate a range of geographical vocabulary.	86 87 88	Rivers and coasts glossary Climate talk Geography debate cards
To use geographical vocabulary in group discussions.	87 88	Climate talk Geography debate cards
To consolidate and use mathematical vocabulary.	90 91 92	The detective and the digit dilemma Explain yourself! Maths trail game
To use vocabulary associated with developing chronological awareness.	94 95	Sorting time Chronology of British history
To consolidate and use a range of historical vocabulary.	96	Top history terms

Observation and record keeping

It can be useful to use colour coding when marking written work. For example, attribute one colour for good vocabulary choices, another colour for useful connectives and a further colour for useful and advanced punctuation. It is important that the scheme is used consistently as part of a marking policy, throughout the year group or Key Stage. Once children are aware of a colour-coding system they can be trained to self-assess their work by using the colour coding to highlight where they have effectively used connectives or powerful verbs and so on. Display examples of useful connectives on a background that matches the colour-coding system for connectives and the same for useful and ambitious vocabulary.

Assessment activity

- **What you need**
Photocopiable page 98 'Cross-curricular connectives', writing materials, poster page 80 'Connectives'.
- **What to do**
Recap the connectives on the poster and reinforce the importance of using connectives in all aspects of writing. Introduce the assessment, which can be used to demonstrate the usefulness of different types of connectives in different curriculum areas. Let the children use the poster to assist them in selecting the most appropriate connective to complete the sentence and then identify which function the connective is performing.

Differentiation

- Highlight the choices on the poster for less confident learners to narrow down the range from which they have to choose.

Further learning

- **Writing:** Encourage the children to write in short bursts to explain concepts in maths or science or to recap evidence for events in history. Encourage them to draw cartoons with speech bubbles to form 'Did you know' facts. When writing these short pieces, encourage them to incorporate the use of connectives.

Name: _____

Assessment

Cross-curricular connectives

■ The sentences below need connectives to join the clauses and sentences together. Using the poster on connectives, choose the most appropriate connective to complete the sentences. Note the group of connectives from which each choice is made.

Science

An irreversible change is a permanent change that cannot be undone,

_____, when we fry an egg it cannot be returned to its raw state.

Connective type: _____.

Mathematics

The mean is an average. To work out the mean, _____ add up all

the numbers in your group. _____ divide the answer by how many

numbers there are. The resulting number is the mean.

Connective type: _____.

History

In Victorian times, 'climbing boys' were boy chimney sweeps who were made to

crawl up chimneys to brush out the poisonous soot. _____ they

were called 'apprentices', they hardly learned anything and led miserable lives.

Connective type: _____.

_____ always being filthy and having permanently grazed knees

and elbows from climbing the chimney walls, climbing boys suffered ill health,

_____ lung disease and 'sooty warts', a form of skin cancer.

Connective type: _____.

Geography

Rivers usually begin life high up on a mountain or hill, high above sea level.

_____, the water has lots of energy as it flows downwards.

Connective type: _____.

_____ rapids and waterfalls, v-shaped valleys are also features of

the upper course of a river.

Connective type: _____.

Word of the week

The Word of the week pages provide information on one word linked to each section in the chapter. Each word is described in some of the following categories: word definition, word origin, word family, alternative words, fascinating facts and activities. Not all categories are relevant to every word.

You can use the words as a focus to support your work on the different sections of the chapter. For example, you could create a display around it. The information is a starting point for a word focus. The words could form part of your classroom living word bank.

You could also use the word of the week as a springboard to inspire children to think about or research fascinating facts about words, find interesting quotations and to encourage them to use dictionaries and thesauruses.

Helicopter

● **Word definition:** A noun meaning an aircraft without wings that obtains its lift from the rotation of overhead blades.
● **Word origin:** From the Greek *helix*, meaning spiral, and *pteron*, meaning wing.
● **Alternative words:** Autogiro, chopper, copter, eggbeater, whirlybird.
● **Fascinating facts:** Leonardo da Vinci was not only an artist but also a great thinker. In the 15th century he conceptualised a machine that could rise into the air by means of a rotating propeller. Monsieur de Ponton in France, in the mid-19th century coined the term *helicopter* from the Greek *helix* and *pteron*.

> Linked section:
> Making sense of science, page 81

Volcano

● **Word definition:** A noun meaning a vent in the earth's crust through which lava, steam and ashes are expelled, either continuously or at irregular intervals; and a mountain or hill, usually having a cuplike crater at the summit, formed around such a vent from the ash and lava expelled through it.
● **Word origin:** From the Latin *vulcanus*, meaning fire.
● **Word family:** Adjective: *volcanic*.
● **Alternative words:** Cleft, crack, crevice, fissure, mount, mountain, opening, vent.

> Linked section:
> A world of words, page 85

● **Fascinating facts:** The ancient Roman god of fire was called Volcanus. To vulcanise rubber means to treat it at a high temperature. The word originally meant to throw into the fire.
● **Activities:** Children can use this word as a prompt for locating famous volcanoes and researching the myths and stories associated with them.

Coefficient

- **Word definition:** A noun meaning the number placed before a letter that represents a variable in multiplying (such as 4x = 8).
- **Word origin:** From the Latin co-, meaning together, and *efficient*, meaning accomplishing.
- **Alternative word:** Constant.
- **Fascinating facts:** Coefficients are used in areas of both maths and science. One thing it is used for is to make sure that things such as planes are aerodynamic.
- **Activities:** This is an example of a word where children may use their knowledge of prefixes and roots to establish the meaning of a word. Set the children mathematical problems, or ask them to create some, which use a coefficient – how many can they solve?

Linked section:
Mastering maths talk, page 89

Marathon

- **Word definition:** A noun meaning a foot race over a course measuring 26 miles 385 yards (42.195 km).
- **Word origin:** From the Greek *Marathon*, an ancient village outside Athens.
- **Word family:** Noun: *marathoner*.
- **Alternative words:** Activity, contest, event, race.
- **Fascinating facts:** The name was given in honour of the soldier Pheidippides who, after the Greeks defeated the Persians in the Battle of Marathon in 490 BC, was given the task of running to Athens to tell them the good news. Tragically, on arrival, totally exhausted, he dropped dead.
- **Activities:** Ask the children to research marathons, perhaps they could write an encyclopedia extract about it.

Linked section:
Defining the past, page 93

Fun with words

. . . .

Use these activities to support the vocabulary work in this chapter. They could be used as starter or plenary activities.

Blagging it

● First choose a curriculum area for the focus of the game. You could choose a topic that you have not yet started, using the game as a means of introducing the new vocabulary.

● Completion of the game will require two sessions. The first session will involve the children, working in groups of three, carrying out research and then writing their questions and false definitions. In the second session the game will be played.

● In the first session, provide the teams with a range of new vocabulary that they are likely to encounter in the chosen forthcoming scheme of work. Give each team two words to work on. This will give a total of about 20 rounds. Ask two members of the team to write a false definition for the word, including pronunciation, information about what part of speech the word is, and an example of the word being used. Ask the other member of the team to write the correct definition, providing the same information as the false definitions. The children should write their word and definition on index cards. Label each definition A, B or C. Ensure the children make the false definitions as credible as possible so it is difficult to decide which definition to choose.

● To play the game, each team should have a name, their cards and a record sheet with the words and A, B C written next to them.

● The first team reads out their word and three definitions. The other teams are given one minute consultation time to decide whether definition A, B or C is correct. They should circle the letter they think is correct next to the word.

● The next team then reads out their first word and definitions and the teams make their choice next to the appropriate word.

● After the teams have all read out their clues, the sheets are swapped around and the true definitions revealed.

● The winning team is the team with the most correct choices.

Chapter 5

Fun with words

Introduction

This final chapter provides fun activities to encourage the children to enjoy the world of words. The activities can be used as warm-up or plenary activities and can be used to lead into literacy work such as poetry and narrative writing, or simply as informative activities to widen vocabulary knowledge.

Poster notes

Terminology town (page 103)
Use the poster to demonstrate examples of the terms and phrases covered in this chapter. Children working at lower levels can use it for support during the assessment activity.

In this chapter

It's delumptious! page 104	To deduce the meaning of made-up words and establish the word class. To use created words in narrative.
Cut it short page 108	To understand the terms *acronym* and *initialism*. To learn the origin and meaning of words that have been shortened or clipped. To experiment with more complex compound words.
Metaphorically speaking… page 112	To consider the meanings of metaphorical expressions and idioms. To have fun explaining and illustrating oxymora.
Splish, splash, whoosh, whizz! page 116	To experiment with onomatopoeia. To expand vocabulary relating to colour words and adjectives.
Assessment page 120	Activities and ideas to assess knowledge of the terms introduced in this chapter.

Fun with words

Terminology town

Can you spot the portmanteau words?

Can you spot the acronyms?

Can you spot the metaphors?

Can you spot the initialisms?

Can you spot the idioms?

BANK of Warwick

ISAs @4%

Hot Soup

Recharge your batteries with a healthy hot soup

Trespassing by arrangement only

Golden Churn
the sunshine spread

Art Gallery

Original copies of famous paintings

WATCHES

Genuine fake watches

MUSIC

SCUBA shop

offers on DVDs

Frobscottle

Get your delumptions
fizzy frobscottle HERE!

Illustrations © 2010, Catherine Ward.

It's delumptious!

To deduce the meaning of made-up words and establish the word class. To use created words in narrative.

Background knowledge

Roald Dahl's *The BFG* (Puffin) oozes with *delumptious* made-up words. There are nouns to describe everyday objects, such as *frobscottle* (a drink), adjectives for descriptions, such as *repulsant* (horrible), and verbs for actions, such as to *swizzfiggle* (tease).

Activities

These activities lead children into Dahl's world, encouraging creativity and experimentation with new vocabulary.

● **Photocopiable page 105 'I is the BFG. Can you talk like me?'**
Discuss Roald Dahl, his books and his success as a children's author. Can the children say what makes his books so popular? Summarise (or invite a child to summarise) the plot and characters in *The BFG*. The BFG's spoonerisms and made-up words provide descriptions that can be so much more fitting than Standard English. Let the children read the quotes and create definitions for the words. They should decide which word class each word belongs to and then attempt to use the words in their own sentences.

● **Photocopiable page 106 'Snozzcumbers and crumpscoddles'**
Fantasy stories use the description of bizarre features to add effect, helping readers to dive further into the fantasy world. In *The BFG*, descriptions of the different giants, *snozzcumbers* and tangible dreams, such as *winksquifflers* and *phizzwizards*, all help to make the reader believe in the place to which Sophie has been *wiggled* away. Ask the children to read the description of the *snozzcumber* and the BFG's reactions to it. Then imagine they are the BFG and give Sophie a description of one of the animals he names that live in Giant country. Encourage the children to give the BFG's opinions of the creature they describe, using made-up words in the same style.

● **Photocopiable page 107 'That's disgusterous'**
Invite the children to make up their own BFG-style words and then create dialogue between Sophie and the BFG to try them out. Many of the words have been created by combining parts of synonyms: *catasterous* is formed from *catastrophe* and *disastrous*. As a class, list all the prefixes and suffixes you can think of and use these to tag on to their created words. Provide thesauruses and suggest a word, such as *horrible*. Create a list of synonyms for children to use to create their own BFG word for *horrible*.

Further idea

● **Made-up dictionary:** Ask the children to scan *The BFG* for further examples of made-up words and create a BFG class dictionary, writing definitions for the words they find and making up other new words to add to it.

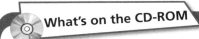 **What's on the CD-ROM**

On the CD-ROM you will find:
● Printable versions of all three photocopiable pages.
● Answers to 'I is the BFG. Can you talk like me?'.

It's delumptious!

I is the BFG. Can you talk like me?

■ Read the list of Roald Dahl's quotes containing made-up words. Write your own interpretation of the word and state whether the word is a verb, noun or adjective. Write a sentence for each of the words to show their use. The first one has been done for you. Note: Questions 4, 5 and 6 all contain three words with the same meaning and word class.

1. "Don't **gobblefunk** around with words."

Meaning	To mess around
Word class	Verb
Sentence	"OK class no gobblefunking around, get on with your work!" instructed the teacher.

2. "I is a nice and **jumbly** giant."

Meaning	
Word class	
Sentence	

3. "You think I is **swizzfiggling** you?"

Meaning	
Word class	
Sentence	

4. "I **squoggle** it! I **mispise** it! I **dispunge** it!" (Describing the snozzcumber, which tastes horrible.)

Meaning	
Word class	
Sentence	

5. "It's **sickable**! It's **rotsome**! It's **maggotwise**!"

Meaning	
Word class	
Sentence	

6. "How **wondercrump**! How **whoopsey-splunkers**! How absolutely **squiffling**!" (After Sophie has told the BFG that she loves the way he talks.)

Meaning	
Word class	
Sentence	

Text extracts © 1982, Roald Dahl.

Name:

It's delumptious!

Snozzcumbers and crumpscoddles

■ Read the description below and underline the adjectives and similes that Dahl uses to describe **snozzcumbers**. In a different colour, highlight the verbs that the BFG uses to describe his feelings towards them.

'I will now show you a snozzcumber.'

The BFG flung open a massive cupboard and took out the weirdest-looking thing Sophie had ever seen. It was about half as long again as an ordinary man but was much thicker. It was as thick around its girth as a perambulator. It was black with white stripes along its length. And it was covered all over with coarse knobbles.

'Here is the repulsant snozzcumber!' cried the BFG, waving it about. 'I squoggle it! I mispise it! I dispunge it!'

■ Sophie has not heard of **humplecrimps**, **wraprascals**, **crumpscoddles** or the **great squizzly scotch-hoppers**. In the book the BFG explains that they are common animals but no descriptions are given.

■ Imagine the BFG takes Sophie to see one of these animals. Choose an animal to describe. Continue the paragraph describing how they approach the animal. Describe what it looks like. How do the BFG and Sophie react? End your paragraph with a sentence of dialogue using made-up words to describe what the BFG thinks about the creature.

"Come on Sophie, I is going to show you a _____" declared the BFG decisively. He whisked Sophie up, placed her in his waistcoat pocket and headed out of the cave.

_____

_____

_____

_____

_____

_____

_____

_____

Text extracts © 1982, Roald Dahl.

PHOTOCOPIABLE **SCHOLASTIC**
www.scholastic.co.uk

It's delumptious!

That's disgusterous

■ Read the BFG's words and their 'translations'.

■ Combine parts of words, root words, prefixes and suffixes to make your own new words. Use the ideas bank to help you.

■ Now have a go at making up some dialogue between Sophie and the BFG on another sheet of paper.

BFG's adjectives

gigantuous – big　　　　　**disgusterous** – disgusting　　**glumptious** – tasty

squimpy – squirmy and wimpy　**catasterous** – disastrous　　**frightsome** – scary

My new adjective: _____

BFG's nouns

rumpledumpus – noise　　　　　　　**bugwhiffles** – strange ideas

chiddlers – a cross between children and toddlers

disastrophe – a cross between a disaster and a catastrophe

My new noun: _____

BFG's verbs

chitter – to chat　　　　　　　**swollop** – to swallow

whizzpop – to pass wind　　　　**swiggle** – to taste

My new verb: _____

Ideas bank

Prefixes	**Nouns**
un- dis- mis- anti- under- sub- mal-	potion medicine concoction
Suffixes	remedy hallucination nightmare
-ful -some -able -ible -ing	delusion trance vision dream
-ous -sy -er -ment	**Verbs**
Adjectives	shock flabbergast stagger
horrible repulsive	astonish daze dumbfound
dreadful staggering horrendous	totter toddle stagger
appalling delicious flavoursome	wobble stumble
appetizing scrumptious yummy	laugh chuckle giggle snigger
juicy succulent funny humorous	cackle snort chortle guffaw
hilarious amusing comical	hoot

BFG words © 1982, Roald Dahl.

Cut it short

To understand the terms *acronym* and *initialism*. To learn the origin and meaning of words that have been shortened or clipped. To experiment with more complex compound words.

Background knowledge

During the 20th century there have been so many new inventions and organisations that we have developed quicker ways of communicating, using abbreviations, acronyms, initialisms, clipped and compound words. Some clipped words are used so frequently that the original word may be forgotten, such as *bus* taken from *omnibus*.

Activities

This section addresses shortened words, names and terms.

● **Photocopiable page 109 'Acronyms and initialisms'**

Acronyms are formed by combining the initial letters of a group of linked words, such as *SCUBA* (self-contained underwater breathing apparatus). An initialism is formed from the initial letters of a series of linked words. It does not form a new word as you pronounce each letter separately, such as *DVD*. Tell the children to match the acronyms and initialisms to their unabbreviated forms. Encourage them to research or discuss the origins of the terms.

● **Photocopiable page 110 'Can you clip? Let me give you a demo'**

Explain that a common way to form new words in English is to shorten existing words by clipping off the front or end of a word. The children may be familiar with the shortened word but do they know the original word? Let the children work in groups or pairs to identify the origins of the clipped words.

● **Photocopiable page 111 'Compound word game'**

Explain that compound words are formed by joining together two words, such as *spellbound*. Copy, laminate and cut up the photocopiable sheet, one per group of four. The children need individual whiteboards, pens, a set of cards, a one-minute sand timer and a judge to keep time and score. Put children in similar ability groups and place the cards face down. Let the players take turns picking two cards to try to make a compound word. When a player makes a compound word they get one point and all players have one minute to write an interesting, accurately punctuated sentence using the word. The judge chooses the winning sentence, awarding that player five points. Play continues until all the pairs have been revealed. The aim is to score the highest number of points.

Further ideas

● **Word tree:** Collect examples of acronyms, abbreviations, initialisms and shortened words on a class word tree. Let the children fill in a leaf when they find examples and stick them on the tree. Encourage the class to look at the tree at the end of the week, rewarding the children who made the best contributions.

What's on the CD-ROM

On the CD-ROM you will find:
● Printable versions of all three photocopiable pages.
● Answers to 'Acronyms and initialisms' and 'Can you clip? Let me give you a demo'.
● Interactive versions of 'Acronyms and initialisms' and 'Compound word game'.

Cut it short

Acronyms and initialisms

■ An acronym is an abbreviation formed from the initial letters of a series of related words. A true acronym can be pronounced as a word.

■ Use the letters of these acronyms to match the acronyms to the unabbreviated form.

■ Research and discuss the origins of these acronyms with a partner.

Acronym	Unabbreviated form
NATO	Double income no kids yet
NASA	Radio detection and ranging
RADAR	National Aeronautics and Space Administration
NIMBY	Self-contained underwater breathing apparatus
SCUBA	Not in my backyard
DINKY	North Atlantic Treaty Organisation
LASER	Light amplification by stimulated emission of radiation
ROM	Personal identification number
PIN	Read-only memory

■ An initialism is like an acronym but the abbreviation does not form a word. Do you know the unabbreviated form of these initialisms?

Initialism	Unabbreviated form
MP	
RSVP	
GP	
CD	
DVD	
ICT	

Name:

Cut it short

Can you clip? Let me give you a demo

- ■ New words are often formed by clipping the beginning or end of a word.
- ■ Write the full version of each of the numbered words in the text into the box below.
- ■ Use a dictionary to help you with the spellings.

My Trip to the Theatre by Charley George

Last week I saw an **1. ad** in the paper for a **2. panto** production of Cinderella at our local theatre. The production was going to star Ben Cartwright, one of my favourite actors – I'm a great **3. fan** of his and I thought it would be **4. brill** to see him on stage. I had only seen him acting on the **5. telly** until now.

Dad said that if I did all my **6. maths** homework on time and got up ready for school promptly so we weren't late for the **7. bus**, then he would buy some tickets for the following weekend. I wrote him a **8. memo** and stuck it on the **9. fridge** so that he wouldn't forget.

The night of the theatre trip arrived. Dad said there was one more condition he had forgotten to mention. I had to eat all my **10. veg** at dinner before we went. This was so unfair. Knowing he was serious, I swallowed down all my carrots, peas and broccoli. (They weren't actually so bad but I wasn't going to let on.)

Soon we arrived at the theatre. A lady made an announcement over the **11. intercom** requesting that everyone took their seats in the auditorium. She reminded everyone that taking **12. photos** was prohibited and requested that all **13. mobiles** were switched off.

The production was great, full of colourful costumes, slapstick comedy and catchy songs. I stood up to applaud when the cast did a final **14. prom** around the stage.

1.	2.
3.	4.
5.	6.
7.	8.
9.	10.
11.	12.
13.	14.

- ■ Can you think of other shortened words? Write them on the back of the sheet.

Cut it short

Compound word game

- You need one set of enlarged and laminated cards per team of four.
- The judge needs the answers and their definitions for reference.

crack	down	draw	back
eaves	drop	eye	witness
fool	proof	more	over
out	cast	spell	bound
proof	read	fore	cast
guess	work	hence	forth
over	all	with	stand

Compound word	Definition
crackdown	A strong measure taken against illegal activities.
eavesdrop	To listen to a conversation without the speakers being aware of it.
foolproof	A plan where failure is thought to be impossible.
outcast	A person who has been rejected by a group.
proofread	To read a text and highlight corrections.
guesswork	Drawing conclusions by making guesses.
overall	Considered as a whole or in general (adverb); or a loose-fitting garment worn over clothes to protect them (noun).
drawback	Something that causes problems.
eyewitness	Someone who was at the scene of an event and can give evidence.
moreover	An adverb used to give extra information in support of a statement.
spellbound	Being totally captivated by something or somebody.
forecast	To predict something that is likely to happen, such as the weather.
henceforth	From now on.
withstand	To have the strength to stand up to something without changing.

Metaphorically speaking...

Objectives

To consider the meanings of metaphorical expressions and idioms. To have fun explaining and illustrating oxymora.

Background knowledge

Metaphors are comparisons that show how two things are similar in one important way. They are a way to describe something. Authors use them to make their writing more interesting. We use metaphorical expressions to describe people, situations or things. Unlike similes that use the words *as* or *like* to make comparisons, metaphors and metaphorical expressions state that something *is* something else.

Idioms are phrases that do not make sense from their literal meaning, but take on a specialised meaning. For example, *barking up the wrong tree* means that someone has got something totally wrong.

An oxymoron is a combination of contradictory or incongruous words, which can be mistakes, but are often created for effect or humour. The word *oxymoron* comes from the Greek *oxy*, meaning sharp, and *moron*, meaning foolish. Examples include *bittersweet* and *same difference*.

Activities

These activities help children to identify different imagery used in text.

● **Photocopiable page 113 'Metaphorical expressions'**

Children will have encountered metaphors as a tool for descriptive writing in poetry and fiction. Explain that a metaphorical expression is a figure of speech where a word or phrase, normally designating one thing, is assigned to another and so an implicit comparison

is made. An example is Shakespeare's *All the world's a stage, and all the men and women merely players*. Discuss the expressions with the children and invite them to make their own suggestions. Can they match the expressions to the situations where they may be used? As a plenary, encourage the children to explain the implicit comparison.

● **Photocopiable page 114 'Just what the doctor ordered!'**

Explain what an idiom is. Suggest that the children imagine they are foreign students trying to learn English. When presented with the phrase *I'm losing my marbles* a student might imagine somebody hunting for marbles. It is only through knowledge of a particular language that we can understand such phrases. Invite the children to identify the hidden idioms in the story. Let them discuss the different meanings or, alternatively, rewrite the story without idioms.

● **Photocopiable page 115 'Are you an advanced beginner with oxymora?'**

Explain what an oxymoron is. Ensure the children understand the meaning of *contradictory*. Give examples and illustrate with drawings if possible. Let the children work in pairs to consider why each of the highlighted phrases is an oxymoron and why they were devised.

Further ideas

● **Dialects:** Invite the children to interview friends and relatives from different parts of the country to give examples of expressions and phrases that are specific to where they are from, or listen to audio files from websites such as http://alt-usage-english.org

What's on the CD-ROM

On the CD-ROM you will find:
● Printable versions of all three photocopiable pages.
● Answers to 'Just what the doctor ordered!'.
● Interactive versions of 'Metaphorical expressions' and 'Are you an advanced beginner with oxymora?'.

Metaphorically speaking…

Metaphorical expressions

■ Cut out the cards and read the metaphorical expressions below with a partner. Write an explanation of the literal meaning of the expression on the back of each card.

Tom is a wizard on the football pitch.

She is the apple of her mother's eye.

He showered her with gifts.

My heart sank.

She was a picture in her ball gown.

Juliet is the sun (from Shakespeare's *Romeo and Juliet*)

His name is mud.

It is just a storm in a teacup.

The vet has a strong stomach.

Illustrations © 2010, Catherine Ward.

Name:

Just what the doctor ordered!

■ Read the story and identify the idioms. Can you replace the idioms and rewrite the story?

It was nearly time for the end-of-year exams. I had really been getting my knickers in a twist over them and making such a terrible fuss that Mum had finally blown her top and I knew I was for the high jump. "You'll lose your marbles if you continue to get so wound up," she said firmly. "Why don't you take stock, and turn over a new leaf? Go and tidy your room, pick up all your books and make everything shipshape and Bristol fashion. Then you will be able to see the wood for the trees and get on with some effective revision."

I crept off with a flea in my ear, but I knew Mum was right. She was pulling rank and there was no carrot and stick approach in her book.

As it was raining cats and dogs outside and my friends were probably all revising, I took Mum's advice and decided to toe the line. The way I had been approaching my exams meant I was on a hiding to nothing and once I had rummaged through the piles of papers and books and organised them into a sensible system I was beginning to see the light. Mum had hit the nail on the head when she had told me that a tidy room meant a tidy mind.

By lunchtime, I had organised all my books into subject piles, sorted out all my pens and pencils and could actually see the keyboard on the computer desk. I had cleared the decks and was now ready to clear the air with Mum.

"Wow, I don't know what to say." Mum declared when she saw my tidy room.

"Has the cat got your tongue Mum?" I asked cheekily, grinning like a Cheshire cat.

Mum gave me a hug and told me to get started on the revision. I got my head down and started with maths. It was going to be so much easier now I was all organised. Two minutes later Mum popped her head around the door, "Here you go, some brain food. This should recharge your batteries," she smiled, "Good luck."

A big bowl of strawberries and cream really was the cherry on the cake!

Illustrations © 2010, Catherine Ward.

Are you an advanced beginner with oxymora?

Oxymoron = **oxy** (sharp) + **moros/moron** (dull or foolish). An oxymoron is a combination of two contradictory words. They are often figures of speech that create a rhetorical effect. For example, a **jumbo shrimp** is an oxymoron because **jumbo** means large and **shrimp** means small.

■ Can you explain these common oxymora?

1. He was so pale he looked like the living dead.

_____

2. The tidal wave was approaching the coast so rapidly that making a run for it was our only choice.

_____

3. "That's a definite maybe," she promised when I asked Sophie if she could come to the cinema on Friday.

_____

4. "Will you sit down and stop talking, it's assembly time." the teacher hissed in a loud whisper.

_____

5. "I've got an original copy of van Gogh's *Sunflowers*," boasted the art collector.

_____

6. There was a deafening silence while the contestants waited to find out who had won the dance competition.

_____

7. "He did it accidentally on purpose Miss, I know he did," whined the Year 2 child when explaining why there was paint all over the cloakroom floor.

_____

8. There was a deliberate mistake on the front page of the paper on April Fool's Day to try to trick the readers.

_____

Splish, splash, whoosh, whizz!

Objectives

To experiment with onomatopoeia. To expand vocabulary relating to colour words and adjectives.

Background knowledge

An *onomatopoeia* (a Greek word meaning name making) is a word that imitates the sound it represents – for example, *buzz*, *gush*, *splash*, *wow* or *whirr*. Exploring and collecting such words can add to a writer's descriptive vocabulary.

Activities

The activities in this section draw attention to how words can be used to create images and sounds in a reader or listener's imagination.

● **Photocopiable page 117 'Can you hear the bells?'**
In the poem, 'The Bells', Edgar Allen Poe's use of onomatopoeia helps the reader to hear the sounds made by different types of bells, such as *tinkling* (sleigh bells), *clanging* (fire bells), *mellow chiming* (wedding bells), and *tolling, moaning, and groaning* (funeral bells). Invite the children to read the first verse of the poem with a talk partner and identify the onomatopoeia. Challenge them to source the poem online and investigate the other bells. Can the children suggest which onomatopoeia could be used to evoke the sound of these bells and give other examples, such as the school bell or door bells?

● **Photocopiable page 118 'Paint your palette'**
The objective of this activity is to broaden the children's knowledge of vocabulary associated with colour. This will increase their repertoire when writing descriptively or composing poems. Let the children use dictionaries to help them to group the different colours. Can they give examples of where they might see the different colours? Invite them to write rainbow poems using the new vocabulary.

● **Photocopiable page 119 'Only 60 seconds'**
Work in two teams for this game. You will need a bag or box to place the cards in. The first team sends up a speaker. When the one-minute timer is begun, they pick a card from the bag and describe it to their team. When the team has correctly guessed, the speaker quickly picks another card. At the end of the minute, record how many items were correctly identified during the round on a scoreboard. To increase the challenge, the speaker must not reveal which group the noun falls into, so you cannot say that it is a vegetable, for example. The game incorporates a range of nouns, but cards could be created on specific topics. If children struggle to describe a specific object, discuss the vocabulary they could have used afterwards.

Further ideas

● **Colour coded:** During an art session let the children mix examples of the different colours on photocopiable page 118 'Paint your palette' to create colour word palettes.

● **On the cards:** Create word cards for photocopiable page 119 'Only 60 seconds' for specific areas of the curriculum, such as characters in Greek mythology or river features in geography.

What's on the CD-ROM

On the CD-ROM you will find:
● Printable versions of all three photocopiable pages.
● Answers to 'Can you hear the bells?' and 'Paint your palette'.
● Interactive version of 'Paint your palette'.

Can you hear the bells?

■ Read the first verse from Edgar Allen Poe's poem out loud with a partner. Highlight the examples of onomatopoeia.

The bells

Hear the sledges with the bells
Silver bells!
What a world of merriment their melody foretells!
How they tinkle, tinkle, tinkle,
In the icy air of night!
While the stars that oversprinkle
All the heavens, seem to twinkle
With a crystalline delight;
Keeping time, time, time,
In a sort of Runic rhyme,
To the tintinnabulation that so musically wells
From the bells, bells, bells, bells,
Bells, bells, bells
From the jingling and the tinkling of the bells.

Edgar Allen Poe

■ Discuss how these words make the reader imagine the sound of the different types of bells and the feelings they stir up.

■ In the other verses of his poem, Poe describes the sounds made by other types of bells. Which words do you think he may have used to create these sounds? Find the poem and see if you were right.

Type of bell	Onomatopoeia used	Feeling it evokes
Wedding bells		
Warning bells		
Funeral bells		

An extract from 'The Bells' by Edgar Allen Poe; illustrations © 2010, Catherine Ward.

Name:

Paint your palette

■ Put each of the colour words on to the correct palette. Use a dictionary to help you with new words.

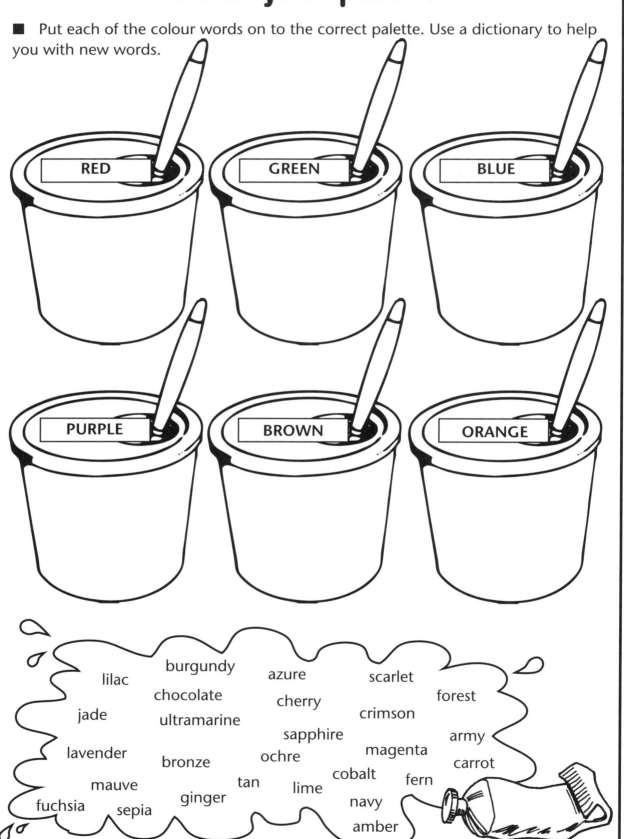

RED   GREEN   BLUE

PURPLE   BROWN   ORANGE

lilac   burgundy   azure   scarlet
chocolate   cherry   forest
jade   ultramarine   crimson
sapphire   army
lavender   ochre   magenta   carrot
bronze
mauve   tan   lime   cobalt   fern
ginger   navy
fuchsia   sepia   amber

Illustrations © 2010, Catherine Ward.

Splish, splash, whoosh, whizz!

Only 60 seconds

■ Cut out these cards and use them to play the **Only 60 seconds** game.

aubergine	mango	kiwi fruit	avocado
yoghurt	rugby	SCUBA diving	hockey
table tennis	golf	walrus	brontosaurus
orang-utan	piranha	llama	tapir
candle	chaise lounge	portcullis	amphitheatre

Illustrations © 2010, Catherine Ward.

Assessment

Assessment grid

The following grid shows the main objectives and activities covered in this chapter. You can use the grid to locate activities that cover a particular focus that you are keen to monitor.

Objective	Page	Activity title
To deduce the meaning of made-up words and establish the word class.	105	I is the BFG. Can you talk like me?
To use created words in narrative.	106 107	Snozzcumbers and Crumpscoddles That's disgusterous
To understand the terms *acronym* and *initialism*.	109	Acronyms and initialisms
To learn the origin and meaning of words that have been shortened or clipped.	110	Can you clip? Let me give you a demo
To experiment with more complex compound words.	111	Compound word game
To consider the meanings of metaphorical expressions and idioms and learn about their origins.	113 114	Metaphorical expressions Just what the doctor ordered!
To have fun explaining and illustrating oxymora.	115	Are you an advanced beginner with oxymora?
To experiment with onomatopoeia.	117	Can you hear the bells?
To expand vocabulary relating to colour words and adjectives.	118 119	Paint your palette Only 60 seconds

Observation and record keeping

Record when children highlight examples of the terms used during guided reading, news sessions and so on, as a record of their cognitive ability to constructively assimilate the learning goals.

Assessment activity

- **What you need**
Photocopiable page 121 'Language lingo', writing materials.
- **What to do**
Children can demonstrate their understanding of the work carried out in this section by providing their own definitions of the terms covered, examples and sentences that demonstrate usage.

Differentiation

- Less confident children may carry out this assessment activity verbally in a discussion group with an adult. You may want to provide examples and invite the children to match them to the terminology.

Further learning

- **Framework:** Incorporate the objectives when teaching the Framework Units, making reference to the taught vocabulary lessons and ensuring the children understand that they are now using the vocabulary lessons in context.

Assessment

Language lingo

■ What is an acronym?

Give an example: _____

Write a sentence using your acronym: _____

_____

■ What is an initialism?

Give an example: _____

Write a sentence using your initialism: _____

_____

■ What is a clipped word?

Give an example: _____

Write a sentence using your clipped word: _____

_____

■ What is a metaphorical expression?

Give an example: _____

Write a sentence using your metaphorical expression: _____

_____

■ What is an idiom?

Give an example: _____

Write a sentence using your idiom: _____

_____

■ What is an oxymoron?

Give an example: _____

Write a sentence using your oxymoron: _____

_____

Word of the week

The Word of the week pages provide information on one word linked to each section in the chapter. Each word is described in some of the following categories: word definition, word origin, word family, alternative words, fascinating facts and activities. Not all categories are relevant to every word.

You can use the words as a focus to support your work on the different sections of the chapter. For example, you could create a display around it. The information is a starting point for a word focus. The words could form part of your classroom living word bank.

You could also use the word of the week as a springboard to inspire children to think about or research fascinating facts about words, find interesting quotations and to encourage them to use dictionaries and thesauruses.

Hassle

- **Word definition:** Trouble or a problem or an argument.
- **Word origin:** This is a portmanteau word dating back to the 19th century made by blending the words *haggle* and *tussle*.
- **Alternative words:** Altercation, argument, bickering, bother, clamour, commotion, difficulty, disagreement, dispute, inconvenience, quarrel, row, run-in, squabble, struggle, trial, trouble, try, tumult, turmoil, tussle, uproar, upset, whirl, wrangle.
- **Fascinating facts:** *Hassle-free* is a term used a lot in advertising.
- **Activities:** Do children use any other colloquial words that are actually portmanteau words, such as *bash* and *smash*?

> **Linked section:**
> It's delumptious!,
> page 104

UNICEF

- **Word definition:** Acronym for United Nations International Children's Fund.
- **Fascinating facts:** UNICEF came about at the end of the Second World War to assist the children in Europe.
- **Activities:** This acronym could be used as a stimulus for finding out about charity organisations and how they work.

> **Linked section:**
> Cut it short,
> page 108

Raining cats and dogs

- **Phrase definition:** Idiom to describe heavy rainfall.
- **Phrase origin:** This expression has several possible origins. Cats are commonly associated with witches who were credited with causing storms. The dogs were associated with the Scandinavian storm god Odin. An alternative explanation dates back to medieval times when dogs and cats roamed the streets. In times of severe flooding, the drowned bodies of these animals may have littered the streets. The people surmised that they had fallen from the skies.
- **Alternative words:** Bucket, come down in buckets, deluge, deposit, downpour, fall, flood, hail, lavish, pour, sleet, storm, thunderstorm.
- **Fascinating facts:** This phrase does not obtain any meaning from cats and dogs falling from the sky. However, other creatures have been known to 'rain', such as frogs and fish.
- **Activities:** Encourage children to use metaphorical expressions in their narrative descriptions of settings, to build atmosphere and create mood.

> **Linked section:**
> Metaphorically speaking…, page 112

Maroon

- **Word definition:** An adjective meaning a dark reddish brown to dark purplish red colour.
- **Word origin:** From the French *marron*, meaning chestnut.
- **Alternative words:** Bloodshot, brick, brown, burgundy, cardinal, carmine, cherry, chestnut, claret, crimson, garnet, geranium, magenta, puce, purple, red, rubicund, ruby, ruddy, russet, rust, sanguine, scarlet, titian, vermilion, wine.
- **Fascinating facts:** A *maroon* is also an explosive signalling device that is used to give a distress signal. This may be linked to the other use of the word as a verb, *to maroon*, which means to leave somebody isolated. This was used to describe what pirates did to their victims on desert islands or it may derive from the disused noun *maroon* meaning a runaway slave.

> **Linked section:**
> Splish, splash, whoosh, whizz!, page 116

Fun with words

Use these activities to support the vocabulary work in this chapter. They could be used as starter or plenary activities.

Spoonerisms
● As well as making up his own words, Roald Dahl used spoonerisms frequently in *The BFG*. Explain to the children what a spoonerism is and invite them to search for examples in Roald Dahl's writing as well as making up their own.

Aptonym
● An aptonym is a name particularly suited to its owner. For example, an aptonym for a barber may be Mr Dan Druff, or a ski instructor may be named Mr Will IT Snow. Challenge the children to create a top ten aptonym chart. There are a number of famous people whose names are appropriate to their jobs, such as William Wordsworth (poet) and Samantha Bond (actress in four James Bond films). Can the children find any more examples?

Animal antics
● The following verbs have a synonym that is also the name of an animal. Can the children detect the animals involved? Put one up on the board during registration. Encourage the class to think of more of their own.
- To outwit: to *fox*
- To strike with great force: to *ram*
- To harass: to *badger*
- To give birth to: to *bear*
- To eat greedily: to *wolf*
- To secure: to *seal*
- To seek something by roundabout means: to *fish*
- To avoid: to *duck*
- To bother: to *bug*
- To gloat or brag: to *crow*
- To imitate: to *ape*
- To rest on an elevated spot: to *perch*
- To persistently harass: to *hound*
- To run about quickly: to *hare*

Word bank

· ·

These word banks, split into three levels of difficulty, relate to the contents of each chapter in the book. Use them for word games and activities to support the learning of the vocabulary in each chapter.

It may be a useful strategy to set up a Vocabulary reward scheme (separate from the school merit scheme) where points are awarded or stars given for good use of target vocabulary, finding examples in texts and so on with a target number of points/stars being rewarded with a prize. To encourage children to strive for higher levels of achievement, allow children the freedom to attempt to work with vocabulary from levels of their choice.

Words from the banks could be displayed as possible target words to use in independent writing – points/stars being earned if used appropriately. Alternatively, children could find meanings and try to incorporate them into a sentence to demonstrate understanding of meaning. Again points/stars would be awarded for children demonstrating a proactive approach to improving their vocabulary.

Children could word process sentences containing the words and highlight or choose a different-coloured font for the target word. Cross-curricular words could be used by children to invent their own Call My Bluff game.

Children could be rewarded for finding examples of each of the target literacy vocabulary.

Synonyms for *said*

Basic	Intermediate	Advanced
asked	enquired	implored
whispered	muttered	murmured
shouted	bellowed	hollered
laughed	giggled	sniggered
gasped	announced	articulate
cried	revealed	pronounced

Powerful verbs

Basic	Intermediate	Advanced
depart	journey	venture
march	amble	saunter
smile	beam	simper
hurry	rush	hasten
gather	assemble	congregate
thought	consider	speculate

Latin and Greek prefixes
Chapter 2

Basic	Intermediate	Advanced
misuse	mislead	misappropriate
unselfish	unconscious	unfortunate
incomplete	inefficient	incompetent
disobey	disqualify	disaffect
immature	impersonal	improbable

Super suffixes

Basic	Intermediate	Advanced
maximum	premium	asylum
minimum	gymnasium	emporium
stadium	geranium	sanatorium
aquarium	planetarium	pandemonium
pendulum	plutonium	harmonium
plectrum	solarium	arboretum

Adverbs
Chapter 3

Basic	Intermediate	Advanced
always	immediately	frequently
early	lately	seldom
soon	persistently	incessantly
continually	barely	scarcely
hardly	advantageously	profitably
usefully	dreadfully	desperately
hopelessly	treacherously	precariously
dangerously	tenderly	compassionately
gently	cautiously	vigilantly
carefully		

Geography vocabulary

Chapter 4

Basic	Intermediate	Advanced
equator	tourism	precipitation
erosion	hemisphere	archipelago
population	topography	abrasion
tropical	peninsula	attrition
glacier	cartography	latitude
terrain	polar	longitude
continent	sediment	meridian

Literacy language
Chapter 5

Basic	Intermediate	Advanced
metaphor	idiom	acronym
simile	imperative verb	cliché
synonym	conditional verb	rhetorical
antonym	personification	imagery
direct speech	causal connective	parody
reported speech	active voice	assonance
connective	passive voice	

Also available in this series:

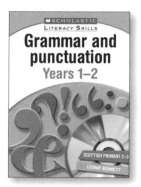

ISBN 978-1407-10045-6

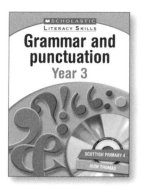

ISBN 978-1407-10046-3

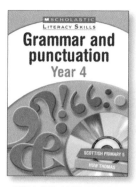

ISBN 978-1407-10047-0

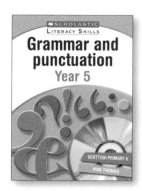

ISBN 978-1407-10048-7

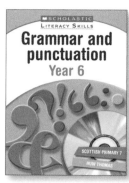

ISBN 978-1407-10049-4

ISBN 978-1407-10055-5

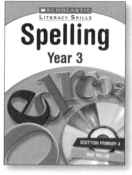

ISBN 978-1407-10056-2

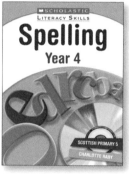

ISBN 978-1407-10057-9

ISBN 978-1407-10058-6

ISBN 978-1407-10059-3

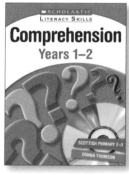

ISBN 978-1407-10050-0

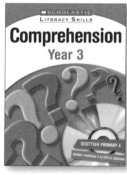

ISBN 978-1407-10051-7

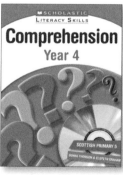

ISBN 978-1407-10052-4

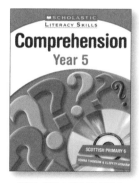

ISBN 978-1407-10053-1

ISBN 978-1407-10054-8

ISBN 978-1407-10223-8

ISBN 978-1407-10224-5

ISBN 978-1407-10225-2

ISBN 978-1407-10226-9

ISBN 978-1407-10227-6

To find out more, call: 0845 603 9091
or visit our website www.scholastic.co.uk